Extraordinary Preaching

Twenty Homilies by Roman Catholic Women

Edited by Roslyn A. Karaban and Deni Mack

Foreword by Walter J. Burghardt, SJ

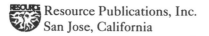 Resource Publications, Inc.
San Jose, California

Editorial director: Nick Wagner
Prepress manager: Elizabeth J. Asborno
Copyeditor: Leila T. Bulling

Reprint Department
Resource Publications, Inc.
160 E. Virginia Street #290
San Jose, CA 95112-5876

Library of Congress Cataloging in Publication Data
Extraordinary preaching: twenty homilies / by Roman Catholic women ;
edited by Roslyn A. Karaban and Deni Mack.
    p.   cm.
    Includes bibliographical references and index.
    ISBN 0-89390-390-6 (pbk.)
    1. Catholic Church—Sermons. 2. Sermons, American—Women authors.
I. Karaban, Roslyn A. II. Mack, Deni (Denise Winfield), 1938- .
BX1756.A2E87 1996
252'.02—dc20   96-30434

Printed in the United States of America

00 99 98 97 96 | 5 4 3 2 1

Pictured on the front cover is Donna Fitch, a graduate of St. Bernard's Institute, Rochester, New York.

To Marie Martin Quinn, RSM
(March 29, 1930-November 28, 1991),
whose life was her greatest homily,
in love and gratitude.

Contents

Foreword ix
    Walter J. Burghardt

Preface xii
Acknowledgments xv

PART 1. Processional

An Invitation 3
    Gloria Ulterino   18th Sunday of the Year (A)
                     Isaiah 55:1-3
                     Romans 8:35,37-39
                     Matthew 14:13-21

"We Are Witnesses to These Things" 6
    Mary Sullivan   Acts 5:27-32
                     Luke 8:40-56

PART 2. Remembering the Women of Scripture: Reclaiming Our Sisters in Faith

Misconceptions of Mary: The Immaculate Conception 15

Roslyn A. Karaban   Feast of the Immaculate Conception
& Martha Ann Sims   Genesis 3:9-15,20
         Luke 1:26-38

The Annunciation 23

Yvonne Lucia   Feast of the Immaculate Conception
         Luke 1:26-38

The Samaritan Woman 26

Kay Heverin   3rd Sunday of Lent (A)
         Exodus 17:3-7
         Romans 5:1-2,5-8
         John 4:5-42

The Canaanite Woman 29

Joan Sobala   20th Sunday of the Year (A)
         Matthew 15:21-28

The Bent-Over Woman 32

Sandra Arrington   Luke 13:10-17

The Adulterous Woman: Gettin' a Twenty-Second Chance . . 38

Toinette Eugene   5th Sunday of Lent (C)
         John 8:1-11

My Sister: A Reflection on Luke 10:38-42 and John 11:1-27 . . 43

Theresa Stanley   Luke 10:38-42
         John 11:1-27

Martha 46

Roni Antenucci   Tuesday of the 27th Week of the Year (II)
         Luke 10:38-42

Mary and Elizabeth 49

Deni Mack   4th Sunday of Advent (C)
         Luke 1:39-45

The Unnamed Woman of Mark 14:3-9:
Mary, Mary, Quite the Contrary! 53
  Roslyn A. Karaban   Mark 14:3-9

PART 3. Uplifting the Women of Today: Celebrating Our Gifts

Celebrating the Gifts of Women: Women's Sunday 61
  Barbara Moore   Ruth 1:8-18
                        Luke 13:10-17

The Banquet of Forgiveness 65
  Donna Ecker   Luke 7:36-50

One Woman's Example: Catechetical Sunday 68
  Mary Britton   24th Sunday of the Year (A)
                        Sirach 27:30-28:7
                        Romans 14:7-9
                        Matthew 18:21-35

How to Be Like Henny Penny 71
  Nancy DeRycke   33rd Sunday of the Year (C)
                        Luke 21:5-19

Saints for Today 74
  Deni Mack   All Saints Day
                        Matthew 5:1-12

Don't Hide Your Gifts in Drawers! 78
  Nancy Giordano   2nd Sunday of the Year (C)
                        Isaiah 62:1-5
                        1 Corinthians 12:4-11
                        John 2:1-12

What Do We Bury in Fear? 81
  Marie Susanne Hoffman   33rd Sunday of the Year (A)
                        Proverbs 31:10-13,19-20,30-31
                        1 Thessalonians 5:1-6
                        Matthew 25:14-30

PART 4. Recessional

We've Only Just Begun... 87
Marie Martin Quinn

About the Contributors 90
Index of Scripture References 95

Foreword

"Sermons by Roman Catholic women?" Isn't this an oxymoron, a contradictory combination, something like "cruel kindness?" In one traditionalist theory, yes indeed. But not in the real world. Catholic women are preaching in increasing numbers, in more and more places, under fresh circumstances but still relatively rarely during the eucharistic liturgy, before the thirty percent of U.S. Catholics who worship regularly on weekends. But it does go on, in retreat houses and priestless parishes, in non-Catholic chapels and at memorial services, and elsewhere.

The present collection of homilies by Roman Catholic women of a single diocese fails to surprise me, though it does delight me. It fails to surprise me because over the last decade I have increasingly come to appreciate the singular gifts women bring to the art and craft of preaching. The appreciation stems not simply from my reading of published sermons but more significantly from

1) hearing women proclaim God's word with striking effectiveness;

2) getting to know women preachers on a more direct, personal level; and

3) listening with rare humility to feminine critiques, gracious but unfailingly frank, of my own efforts from the pulpit.

Though not surprised by this collection, I am indeed delighted. What is it that comes from these female preachers and is all too often (not always) missing from our male clergy?

1) Concreteness coupled with imagination: in language, in stories, in use of contemporary as well as biblical symbols.

2) Ability to link rich, at times profound, understanding of Scripture with current issues, cultural and individual; reconstruction of the Bible's cultural and historical milieu so as to hear God's message addressed to us today.

3) Awareness that the Word of God is addressed in the first instance to the preacher.

4) Realization that the outcome, the effect, depends not so much on the preacher's gifts as on the relationship between God and the individual listener.

Then, impressively, there are insights into the Gospels that ordinarily escape even the most insightful of males. A handful of examples from this collection must suffice: a personal experience of our Lady not only through prayer and reflection but from experience of pregnancy, of commitment to a husband, of family life, of maternal and wifely suffering, and of letting go; an experience of Mary moving through fear and confusion to transformation; an experience of Mary and Elizabeth needing each other, each discovering what God is doing in the other's life as well as her own. In freeing the Samaritan woman to be herself, Jesus tells us to risk being who we really are, to acknowledge our own sin, to move on. From the Canaanite woman to whom Jesus seems so uncommonly insensitive, Wisdom-in-flesh himself learns a bit of wisdom. In an unnamed town, in an obscure house of worship, an anonymous woman becomes a sign of God's reign. This bent-over woman, doubly outcast by gender and bodily deformity, is empowered in the midst of the assembly to "stand tall" as a person loved, is set free to be. To an adulteress, cards hopelessly stacked against her by unilateral sexism, Jesus restores human dignity. And there is the homilist playing the part of Martha, thinking aloud the thoughts of Martha, our sister in busy-ness, distracted by oh so many things—e.g., visitors like Jesus who need to eat.

And there are the contemporary stories, stunning, surprising. The two women, Linda, older and ugly, Tina, (once) beautiful, fighting repeatedly, in love with the same manipulating pimp—and the younger woman's wrenching prayer for forgiveness: "I know we ain't never going to be friends. But we shouldn't be enemies." (Tina was murdered on the streets of Rochester.) Then, too, the depth of meaning underlying a little girl's willingness to save her lovely new pajamas for a better occasion, only to find all too soon she has outgrown them. Our gifts, like wine, are to be used, to be enjoyed, to be...shared.

Nothing bland about these homilies. They are ceaselessly provocative, sure to exasperate the hidebound and occasionally the intelligently sophisticated, but always encouraging, uplifting, urging us to be free, graced men and women the Son of God took our flesh to shape.

I have but one regret: that "the days of our life are seventy years, or perhaps eighty if we are strong" (Ps 90:10). In that context, I shall not experience the day when women preach the Gospel with the same freedom I have enjoyed for over half a century. "Alas, poor Yorick!"

Walter J. Burghardt, SJ

Preface

There are many collections of homilies[1]—some well worth the purchase price, and others not as worthwhile. Why, then, put together yet another collection? What is special about this collection that would set it apart from the already numerous collections? Although there are at least a few good collections of sermons by women,[2] there doesn't yet seem to be a collection of homilies that is exclusively by Roman Catholic women. That, then, is the first distinctive quality of this collection: it is totally by Roman Catholic women, a fact well worth noting since it is commonly believed that Roman Catholic women don't or can't preach. The second distinctive quality is that this is a collection of homilies by Roman Catholic women who are from one Roman Catholic diocese. No effort was made to reach the best Roman Catholic women preachers in the country so that it might be shown that a few Roman Catholic women can and do preach and preach well. In other words, if this is the quality and the quantity of preaching occurring from women within one diocese, imagine what is and/or could be happening throughout the country and the world.

The final distinctive quality of this collection is that it means to respond to the unspoken question that lurks in the recesses of many Roman Catholic minds and often finds its way to the heatedly spoken word: Can Roman Catholic women preach? This question is really two questions:

1. Are women *capable* of doing so? (a question of *competency*)

2. Are women *allowed* to do so? (a question of *authority*)

These questions are not really questions about women per se but about lay people in particular. However, the question "Can lay people preach?" has become primarily a question of "Can lay *women* preach?" probably because of the predominance of women in lay ministries. Interestingly enough, many of the women who are preaching would prefer to be doing so as ordained clergy. The editors of this book, while appreciating this perspective, do not want to disregard the importance of promoting *lay* preaching, regardless of the tomorrow when women will be ordained.

This book stands as a testimony to a positive response to both versions of the question, "Can Roman Catholic women preach?" This book is a collection of high-quality homilies that were preached by Roman Catholic women who were asked and authorized to preach. We believe not only that Roman Catholic women can preach but that they are *extraordinary* in their ability to do so.[3] We, the church, the people of God, have been experiencing the extraordinary preaching of Roman Catholic women for a number of years now. We have been ministered to, been uplifted, and have drawn closer to God because of this preaching. This book is but one testimony to this.

Some Comments on the Homilies

The twenty homilies selected for this book represent a wide variety of preachers and preaching settings. The model of preaching that is used is preaching from a woman's perspective, particularly a *lay* woman's perspective.[4] This perspective means preaching from one's inner voice, preaching from experience, using imagery and story, and speaking of God in the particular. The homilies gathered here get close to the needs of the human heart. These lay women preachers concretize their message. They break open the Word in relation to the way they experience life. They preach in a variety of settings and from a variety of experiences. Women such as Karaban and Sullivan bring their academic backgrounds into their preaching while a more pastoral perspective is evident in such homilies as those by Heverin, Sobala, Ecker, and DeRycke. A more poetic use of imagery is found in Stanley's reflection as well as in Arrington's homily. Story and experience are found in most every homily, especially in Mack and Britton. Sullivan and Eugene explicitly deal with themes of oppression and justice. All homilies are invitations, and Ulterino even titles hers as such. There is a lack of competitiveness in the preaching and the listener/reader is left with a profound sense of having been allowed to share deeply in the living word. We see that in speaking as lay people who live and work in the world the homilists talk about the stories and problems of the world.

We hope that you will enjoy reading these homilies as much as we have enjoyed gathering and editing them. It has been a labor of love. May you receive them in that spirit.

NOTES

1. In the Roman Catholic tradition, the message preached after the Gospel is referred to as the "homily." Therefore, in this collection, the word "homily" is used to refer to this message.
2. Collections of sermons by women include: David Albert Framer and Edwina Hunter, eds., *And Blessed Is She: Sermons by Women*, San Francisco: Harper and Row, 1990; Charles D. Hackett, ed., *Women of the Word: Contemporary Sermons by Women Clergy*, Atlanta: Susan Hunter Pub., 1985; Annie Lally Milhaven, ed., *Sermons Seldom Heard: Women Proclaim Their Lives*, New York: Crossroad, 1991; Ella Pearson Mitchell, ed., *Those Preachin' Women: Sermons by Black Women Preachers*, Valley Forge: Judson Press, 1985; Ella Pearson Mitchell, ed., *Those Preachin' Women: More Sermons by Black Women Preachers*, Valley Forge: Judson Press, 1988.
3. According to canon law (canons 762, 764, 767), the usual or *ordinary* preacher is a presbyter or deacon. Therefore, when a non-ordained person preaches, the circumstances may be considered *extraordinary* ("certain circumstances," canon 766); thus, preaching by a lay person would be extraordinary by virtue of circumstance. In naming this book *Extraordinary Preaching*, we mean to say that the preaching is extraordinary not only according to canon law but also by virtue of its quality.
4. One might argue that the characteristics that we attribute to these homilies also define feminist preaching (see Christine M. Smith, *Weaving the Sermon: Preaching in a Feminist Perspective* [Louisville: John Knox Press, 1989]). However, in gathering homilies, we did not ask women to submit feminist homilies but those homilies which they liked or which were representative of their specialized ministry. Therefore, we are calling these homilies "homilies written from a lay woman's perspective" rather than "homilies written from a feminist perspective."

Acknowledgments

This book comes to completion for us—more than six years after it was begun—with the writing of a note of thanks to the various people who have walked with us throughout this long and sometimes arduous journey.

We thank:

- all the women who contributed homilies to this book, our sisters in faith, who spent long hours translating their oral message into the written word; you have truly been our companions on the journey;

- our beloved bishop, Matthew, who has supported us from the beginning and who continues to be an inspiration to us;

- our families and friends, particularly Prem, Deepa, Micah, Ron, Therese, Brian, Steve, and Deirdre, the children-in-law and grandbabies, who have lived with us and loved us as we have despaired and rejoiced throughout the last six years;

- Walter Burghardt, preacher par excellence, who read our manuscript and agreed to write our foreword before ever meeting us and whose enthusiasm for our work continues to amaze and uplift us;

- our endorsers, whose kind words of praise have renewed our spirits;

- Diana Moore and Joanne Popeck, who proofread the text for grammar and style;

- St. Bernard's Institute and Roslyn's colleagues there for their constant and continued faith in her abilities and their support in her ministry and in particular to President Patricia Schoelles for helping to make possible a sabbatical to complete this book;

- the people of St. Anne's, St. Gregory's, St. Catherine's, St. Rita's, Corpus Christi, and Church of the Holy Name who have shown Deni the many faces of God;

- our publisher, Resource Publications, Inc., who believed in us when other publishers lacked the courage and vision to publish what might be considered provocative or controversial;

- Nick Wagner, our editor, for his unending patience, unceasing concern, and unfailing wisdom and guidance; he has been a joy to work with, a gracious blessing in our lives;

- Elizabeth Asborno, our prepress manager, for her layout of our final manuscript;

- and finally, to our colleague and friend, Deni's partner in ministry, Sister Marie Martin Quinn, who died suddenly shortly after this project began, and to whom—in gratitude and with love—we dedicate this book.

PART 1

Processional

Isaiah 55:1-3
Romans 8:35,37-39
Matthew 14:13-21

An Invitation

Gloria Ulterino

Summertime is often a time of parties and of invitations to parties. I couldn't help thinking of that as I reflected on the first reading today from Isaiah. What if Isaiah's invitation came to us today in the mail? My imagination tells me we might find something like this:

You Are Invited

To a Party:	Of Life
Informal:	Come as you are: hungry, tired or refreshed, lonely, running on empty, or on top of the world
Only Requirement:	You will want to come. You will settle for nothing less than real life.
Cost:	Absolutely free of charge.
When:	Now
RSVP:	Directly to God (1-800-7-heaven) or Through the Body of Christ
PS:	This invitation has no limits.

God sent this invitation—or one very much like it—over and over again to the people of Israel. In this reading, God sent it through the prophet Isaiah. But few accepted this invitation to life.

So God tried again—this time in human flesh, in Jesus. And Jesus became, in his person and his whole way of living, that invitation to life that has been a model for all of us as Christians. We call it Eucharist. Jesus took bread—something very ordinary and "not enough" at that (only five loaves)—offered it to God for a blessing, broke it open, and gave it to his disciples to share. People were fed and Eucharist happened; and there was more than enough left over, besides. How did Jesus know about this eucharistic action, this invitation to life? Maybe because he knew what it felt like to be ordinary, to be "not enough," to be human. He knew the limits as well as the magnitude of humanness.

The Gospel story opens with a Jesus who is feeling the depth of his humanity, who doesn't "have it all together." He has just heard of the death of John the Baptist, the murder of his cousin, and he needs to be alone. To grieve? Perhaps. To reflect on his own mortality? Perhaps. To come to terms with the sure knowledge that he might be next? Possibly. But surely to experience the depths, the vulnerability, the limits of his humanness. Surely to identify his pain with the pain and the limits of those in the crowd. And surely to see the possibilities of God's humanity shared. How true it was! All his disciples could see were the limits, the "not enough" to go around. But Jesus knew better. So, taking only the five loaves, he offered it to God for a blessing, broke it open and gave it to those same disciples to share. People were fed and Eucharist happened; and there was more than enough, besides.

But *how* did this happen? Through magic? Not likely—Jesus never was into magic. More likely through a look, a look of invitation that could uncover a loaf of bread that someone had stashed away in selfishness here or there. A look of confidence and acceptance that clearly said to each heart: "I know and understand. There is enough, right here in this crowd, among all of you. Believe it and you will see it." The invitation to life was accepted. People were fed and Eucharist happened.

God still offers us the same invitation to life—in human flesh—through the Body of Christ, and we still name it Eucharist. It is bread offered to God, blessed, broken and shared. All are fed and Eucharist happens, here in this assembly and beyond in our daily lives. A friend cares, listens, suggests that maybe you are running yourself ragged in an effort even to do good; maybe a better way to care can be found. The truth is recognized and both church family and wider community are fed and Eucharist happens. Social ministry people meet and passionately search for ways to advocate for the homeless and the poor. People are fed and Eucharist happens.

Yes, God sends us this invitation every day through the Body of Christ. We only need to want it. We can still respond directly to God or through the Body of Christ; it really doesn't matter. Whenever and however we accept this invitation, people will be fed and Eucharist will happen.

Acts 5:27-32
Luke 8:40-56

"We Are Witnesses to These Things"

Mary C. Sullivan, RSM

Preached for Church Women United Preaching Festival

Witness to whom? Who needs to hear our words and God's Word?

I have lived with and struggled with the vocation of this moment for many reasons:

- because none of us who have preached or will preach today wants our homilies to be simply performances in a series of performances at a Preaching Festival;

- because the relationship between preacher and hearers is the most mysterious of all ministerial relationships, its outcome wholly dependent on the relationship between God and the individual hearers—a relationship which the preacher may or may not assist with but which she can never create or prevent;

- because I do not know many of you; we are not together, a continuing community, and I do not directly serve with you and walk with you in my daily

life: I am sort of dropped in your midst—like some
unknowing Habakkuk (if he ever *was* dropped
anywhere except among God's oppressed people);

And, I have struggled with the obligation of this moment
because I always feel phony about "one night Christian stands,"
when I cannot on the morrow, in any tangible way, pick up with
you our common tasks and work with you at the real preaching of
which any sermon or homily is only a word of encouragement from
the sidelines.

So I open my mouth here tonight humbly, hoping deeply that
somehow God will allow these moments to be blessed for you in
some way that I cannot know and that Christ will give you some gift
of courage, faith, hope, or love that will be a blessing for you and for
God's people.

We ask ourselves tonight:

- To whom do we witness?

- Who needs to hear our words and God's word?

My answer to that question is very simple:

- first, ourselves,

- and then all those with whom we suffer.

As we begin to understand what this means, I ask you please to
come with me, to get lost with me, in the crowd outside Jairus's
house, and to keep your eye, as I'm trying to keep mine, on the
poor woman who is slowly moving up behind Jesus—the one with
the continuous hemorrhage, bearing all the distress, awkwardness,
and insecurity that trouble entails.

I long ago began to realize that the truthfulness, and therefore,
the agony of preaching, and of preparing to preach, arises from the
Christian fact that the word of God is *first* of all addressed to *me*, and
if

my so-called preaching,

my so-called witnessing

is going to be, by the grace of God, of any ancillary help or benefit
to others, I have somehow to preach to myself even as I struggle to
preach to them—and to you.

What this means is that, as I stand in that crowd,

- I have to try earnestly to hear what the word of God is saying to *me*—not just what the words of the specific scriptural text are saying to me but what God is saying to me—through the whole of God's word and the whole of *my* "Sitz im Leben" ("situation in life").

- The words I use when I preach, when I try to witness to God's loving activity in our lives and world, have to make sense to me and have to be received by *me*—I can't just put them on paper or fix them in my memory or say them without welcoming them into *my mind* and *my heart* and *my daily life*—welcome them at least today, even though tomorrow I may thoughtlessly or fearfully or selfishly fall away from that welcoming.

- I have to hear myself what I wish to preach to others; *I* have to sit before the very words God asks me to utter to others and listen to them myself with earnest desire to receive and surrender to what God is saying to me and asking of me.

I cannot, in any Christian sense, be "a witness to these things" (Acts 5:32a) if I have not somehow let God bear witness in me, to me:

- I cannot preach God's mercifulness if I do not at the same time listen to God's word in my own poor words, and hear and embrace that same mercifulness in my own sloppy, fumbling being.

- I cannot preach God's solidarity with the sick and dying, the poor and oppressed, if I do not myself listen to God's word in my own poor words and search for truer, deeper solidarity with the sick, the poor, and the oppressed.

- I cannot preach the meaning, the obedience, the mystery, the daring, the attentiveness, the surrender that we call "prayer" if I do not, myself, listen to God's word in my own poor words and try to let the spirit of God pray in me, with all the peculiar pleas, wordlessness and weakness that may be the spirit's prayer in me.

Oh, I can stand before the crowd and rattle on, as a preacher—and I can pile up great phrases and wonderful images in my preaching; and I can do and say all the right things—all the things the books say good preachers do and say; and I can sound terrific in a preacherly sort of way and people in the crowd can say, "My, that was a wonderful homily!"

But if I do not preach first to myself and if I do not listen myself to the word God may be trying to say to others through my own poor words, then I do not think those others will be able to hear that word of God in any deep and lasting way.

And so we come back to the woman with the hemorrhage—the woman in the crowd who reaches out to try to touch the fringe of Jesus' garment (Luke 8:40-48)—a woman driven to Jesus by desperate need.

I see in this woman the image of all who try to preach in Jesus' name, of all who try, in faltering but deliberate ways to share their confidence in the saving activity of God in the midst of the great and pressing crowd who are God's people:

Somehow, having listened, having dared to reach out to Jesus, she realizes that power has gone forth from him, to her; and at Jesus' word,

She, the unlikely preacher, comes forward trembling, and falling down before him, declares in the presence of all the people why she has touched him and how surely she has been healed.

This nameless woman, with all her embarrassments and all her misunderstandings about the true nature of Jesus' power, nonetheless, reaches out to him and healed proclaims his goodness.

She preaches *to herself* and *to others* in the crowd with whom she suffers.

And that crowd of all those with whom we suffer, with whom we are in solidarity, they, finally, are the ones to whom we witness: the ones who—we dare presume to say—need to hear our words and God's word.

After we have preached to ourselves, in whatever ways are real and deep for us, we have to declare God's word in the presence of all the people; we have to open our mouths with compassion for the multitude; we have to speak God's word to all those with whom we suffer, to all those with whose suffering we are in solidarity.

We cannot preach God's gracious word of hope and compassion to those who suffer—from a space of immunity, from a distant place, from a detached study or pulpit.

We can preach to those who suffer

- only if they are those *with whom* we suffer;

- only if we are in genuine solidarity with them in their suffering;

- only if we have stood with them and felt with them, and hungered and hoped with them, and jostled in the needy, waiting crowd with them;

- only if we have for them that limitless, precarious, vulnerable affection and benevolence which is authentic love;

- only if we are, like Jesus Christ, moved with compassion for their redemption: their healing and their joy.

Then, somehow, Christ in us can reach out and touch them, can say something to and about them.

Then, somehow, Christ in us can preach to and about the multitudes who knowingly or unknowingly strain toward him, come up behind him, reach out to touch him:

- the paralytics,

- the blind,

- the widowed,

- the withered,

- the Canaanite women,

- those on the thoroughfares,

- the fishermen,

- the lepers,

- the hungry,

- the homeless,

- the people on public assistance,

- the grieving,

- those dying of AIDS,

- those hemorrhaging from alcohol, corporate success, discouragement, sexual and racial putdowns,

- youth who feel unwanted,

- aging folks who feel useless,

- *whoever* suffers, *wherever, however.*

We are sent to witness to the same people Jesus was sent to and Christ is sent to: the whole crowd of those who suffer, with whom and in whom we suffer.

We are called to witness, yes, first, privately, to ourselves that we may believe and have confidence in the midst of our common and our particular afflictions and then, we are called to witness publicly, lovingly, bravely, tenderly to all those who stand outside and inside the Sanhedrin, to all those who weep and mourn inside Jairus' house.

And we are called to do so as Jesus the Christ did and does:

> For we have not a high priest who is unable to sympathize with our weaknesses, but one who in every respect has been tempted as we are, yet without sin. He can deal gently with the ignorant and wayward, since he himself is beset with weakness (Heb 4:15, 5:2).

The woman with the hemorrhage came to know this.

We, too, must come to know it and then share the truth and hope of it with those whose suffering we come to understand as our own.

I pray this redeeming gift of compassion for myself and for each of you.

PART 2

Remembering the Women of Scripture: Reclaiming Our Sisters in Faith

Genesis 3:9-15,26
Luke 1:26-38

Misconceptions of Mary: The Immaculate Conception

Roslyn A. Karaban and Martha Ann Sims

Preached at All-School Worship, Colgate Rochester Divinity School/Bexley Hall/Crozer Theological Seminary and St. Bernard's Institute

Mary in Tradition and Scripture

Roslyn A. Karaban

P eople who have heard me preach or speak or who have had class with me have discovered at least two things about me: I like to begin with stories or nursery rhymes and I like the word "misconceptions." True to form, I have included both today. The homily title contains the word "misconceptions" and I will begin with a story. This is a story cited by Mary G. Durkin in a volume of *Chicago Studies.* Ms. Durkin relates a story that her mother had told her about a meeting her mother attended during Ladies Week at a Parish Mission in the 1940s:

> The visiting preacher, true to his "hell, fire, and brimstone" reputation, sought to impress the ladies with their responsibilities as

wives and mothers. Their children were going astray because the
mothers didn't imitate the Blessed Virgin Mary. All of his listeners'
failures as mothers seemed even worse compared to the virtues of
the virgin as he described them. She always did God's will. She
never lost her temper with the child Jesus. She kept a neat house.
She waited on Joseph and her son. She prayed constantly. On and
on, for forty-five minutes, the preacher chastised the women for
their failures while at the same time reminding them that they
would never be as good as Mary because they were sinners and she
was not. Their only hope was to pray to Mary to help them overcome
their sinfulness. As the women filed out of the church after the
closing benediction, my mother's friend, the mother of six, said in a
stage whisper, "Sure, and it was easy enough for her. She only had
one child and he was God" (16-17).

So much for Mary being a model for us! The Mary of this story is
beyond our experiences of parenting. She is extolled as a perfect
ideal, beyond our mere mortal possibilities as she is totally without
sin, always obedient, endlessly patient, a perfect housekeeper, and
an ever faithful servant to God, Joseph, and Jesus. This is an
interpretation, and I would say *misconception* of Mary, that many of
us grew up with, and in the sweeping reforms of Vatican II, it is an
image that we long since have rejected. Yet, in rejecting this image,
we have perhaps not taken sufficient time and imagination to
explore other possible Mary images. *I* certainly have not taken the
time to do so. Today I invite you to take some time with me to take
another look at Mary and to imagine her anew; and since today,
December 8, was declared the Feast of the Immaculate Conception
by Pope Pius IX in 1854, it would be appropriate to look at least at
this one teaching concerning Mary and how it has informed our
image of her.

At first glance, or first hearing, we might think that the term
"immaculate conception" refers to Jesus' conception —that Jesus
was immaculately conceived without sin. And considering the
passage from Luke's Gospel that we just heard which is part of the
lectionary readings for today (Lk 1:26-38), this would seem like a
logical conclusion to draw. However, the Feast of the Immaculate
Conception does *not* refer to Jesus' conception, but to Mary's.

In an 1854 document, "Ineffabilis Deus," Pope Pius IX defined
the Immaculate Conception as a dogma of faith, saying that Mary
was without original sin from conception. This decree was founded

at least in part on a passage from Genesis (Gen 3:15), that forms part of the lectionary readings today, and partly on Gabriel's pronouncement in Luke: "Hail, O favored one, the Lord is with you!" (Lk 1:28b)

The doctrine of the Immaculate Conception also developed through centuries of debate among church leaders. The earliest church leaders regarded Mary as holy but not as absolutely sinless. The Council of Ephesus in the year 431 ratified Mary's title as "Mother of God, God-Bearer, Theotokos." And by the eighth century, her holiness and sinlessness were highly esteemed in the East and in the West by the eleventh century. As far as the celebration of a feast day in honor of Mary and her sinlessness, a feast began to be celebrated before the year 700; the feast reached England around the year 1050 and was revived in 1125. At first, the argument centered on whether it was right to *celebrate* the feast and only incidentally on the question or issue of an immaculate conception. Most of the eminent theologians of the Middle Ages (including St. Bernard) denied that Mary was conceived without sin while holding that she was freed from original sin before her birth. It was Duns Scot, a Franciscan, who in the thirteenth century argued that Mary was without sin from the moment of conception but that she is still dependent on Christ's redemptive work. This view was seen to be in conformity with the prevalent doctrine of universal redemption and was therefore an acceptable compromise position and one which turned the tide in favor of belief in an immaculate conception.

However, we as modern Christians, more than one hundred years after the decree of Pius IX and many hundreds of years after the arguments and controversies surrounding the doctrine, have little awareness of the process involved in decreeing Mary as immaculately conceived. For us, "immaculately conceived" holds a meaning often devoid of an understanding of what lies behind that meaning and may even represent a misconception of the intended meaning. For some of us, the term "immaculate conception" conjures up an image of a pure, sinless, semi-divine virgin, so unlike the tainted and sinful and very human beings that we are, as to be incomprehensible. We may understand a doctrine of an immaculately conceived Mary to focus on the perfection of Mary, while ignoring, or at least undermining, the importance of the personhood of Mary and of women in general. With such an understanding, we may have a tendency to reject the doctrine and with it Mary. In so doing, however, I fear we have thrown the baby out with the bath water (or in this case we have thrown the baby's mother out with the bath water.)

If we agree that we do not really want to go this far, what then can we do? How can we understand the Mary of the Immaculate Conception? Stated quite simply, this Mary is a woman of grace as all Christians are by virtue of their baptism. Mary just received her grace a little sooner than the rest of us. To say that she was immaculately conceived may be to say that Mary received at the moment when her soul was infused into her body, the graces all Christians normally receive at baptism. Perhaps, however, this is an image that still does not appeal to you. I would suggest that this image should not be considered in isolation. We need to consider the doctrine and the Mary of the doctrine of the Immaculate Conception in its entire historicity (herstoricity), and we need also to explore what images Scripture and experience give us of Mary, in order to derive or formulate a more comprehensive and holistic image of Mary.

Luke 1:26-38 is referred to as the annunciation, the angel Gabriel announcing to Mary that she is to be the mother of the most high, Jesus. The Mary of these verses is the object of God's grace and favor. Mary responds to this favor initially by questioning, and only after questioning, does she accept the announcement in faith. We have here a Mary who as the future mother of Jesus will enjoy a prominent position in Christian history and in the Christian church. In this passage, however, Mary is not yet mother, and according to Luke, it is not her physical motherhood that is important. We need only to remember Luke 11:27-28 to see that Mary's importance is that she is one who hears the word of God with perseverance and belief and does it: "As he said this, a woman in the crowd raised her voice and said to him, 'Blessed is the womb that bore you, and the breasts that you sucked!' But he said, 'Blessed rather are those who hear the word of God and keep it!'" This emphasis of Luke on Mary's response, rather than on her physical being or physical motherhood, lends another perspective to our imaging of Mary.

Neither the doctrine of the immaculate conception, nor Luke's scriptural depiction of Mary in the annunciation, however, paint a complete picture of Mary for us, and the images of Scripture and tradition are often—even at their best—misinterpreted and misunderstood. I believe that there needs to be another dimension added to our imaging of Mary, and this is our own personal experience of Mary—informed by Scripture and tradition, certainly, but also experienced in our personal relationship with Mary through prayer and reflection. Martha Ann will speak about this dimension.

Reflections on Mary

Martha Ann Sims

By way of preparing you for any presuppositions which you might hear, I want to tell you that I am a product of twelve years of Catholic parochial education, a child of Catholic Irish and Polish parents. Though my early education took place in the Southwest, where the winds of democratic and independent thinking blew strongly enough to penetrate even the classrooms and sanctuaries of the church, still I retain many peculiarly "Catholic" images, not all of which have been looked at by me in light of modern catholicity and my own maturing process.

Mary As a Porcelain Model

Though indirectly from home, but certainly and clearly from the sisters who taught me in school, I was introduced to Mary at an early age as an ideal of piety and goodness and model for girlhood and young womanhood. I accepted this model wholeheartedly. Mary had meaning for me as someone to look to as I made my childhood choices—to pray, to commit myself to daily mass, to do what was expected of me.

But upon entry into the world of young adulthood, of adolescence with its myriad of uncertainties, the model of Mary as sheltered virgin and prayerful daughter became increasingly remote. As I moved into the grownup world of independent living, teaching, marriage, and motherhood, these images of Mary seemed as lifeless as the porcelain statues which depicted her. She did not seem to connect with the lives of my junior high students in their struggles with academic achievement or lack of it, in their blossoming and burgeoning adolescence, or their family and peer problems. A few years later, amidst the endless buckets of diapers and sleepless nights nursing infants, and in the challenges of living in a relationship of love and responsibility with another, I found Mary's model of piety and virginity both inappropriate and irrelevant.

Mary Enfleshed

Not until age forty, when I was pregnant with my fifth child, did I begin to hear the readings about Mary and Jesus in new ways. As my oldest two children entered their teens and the new worlds outside our home, they and others who knew them began to reflect back to me new and surprising understandings of who they were. These reflections were sometimes startlingly different from my own perceptions of them, challenging my visions and expectations for them, as well as my ways of parenting. I began to realize that they were not far from entering the world as unique and independent persons, mysteries in their own right, as individuals created and loved even more by God than by me. In a search for a model in these letting-go's, I began to see Mary differently. Now my thoughts about her motherhood were full of questions about *her* letting-go's and her loving with patience and wisdom. I began to look at her with feelings of commiseration. She was coming down from the pedestal as the perfect woman, and becoming a peer in relationship.

Questions which I had never heard before spoke to me from the Scripture readings about Mary. Who was she as mother of this child who stayed behind in the Temple to talk to the teachers, without telling anyone? And before that event, who was Mary as she pondered the unknown future of her infant—whose birth was a sign to shepherds and kings and the object of prophecy by Simeon and Anna? Who was she as Jesus left home and community to become a preacher calling for radical religious and political change? Who was she as middle-aged mother, grieving the sufferings and death of her son, and in this searching for the meaning of his life?

From Mary as mother, it was but a small step to ponder Mary as spouse. How did she live out in faithfulness and love her commitment to Joseph, a gentle and faithful man, grounded in the practical realities of life as I think carpenters must be? Who was she as a Jewish wife? What were the constraints and restrictions which her culture imposed on her ability to grow to the fullness of her potential? As I reflected on the practicalities and responsibilities of her ordinary life, I concluded that life with Joseph and Jesus had to be more complex than the stained glass windows and Christmas cards depict. In these reflections on Mary, as wife and mother, came the dawning of a new awareness that marriage offered the potential for growth to holiness and wholeness, even to sainthood. I no longer visualized the holy family as always gathered in serenity. Now I could relate my struggles in intimate community and interpersonal relationships to what had become, at last, a living model from Scripture.

In the church's doctrine of Mary's Immaculate Conception, I now understand the image of this woman's total though gradual saying yes to God. She is a model of singleness of heart. She was destined to say "Yes" to God, and in the freedom of her human situation and choices, she lived out that destiny. We have a similar destiny—to live a life of saying "Yes" to God, yes to the truth of our own creation and becoming, as we discover it in life's circumstances, whatever they may be.

In the absence of the feminine in the theology of the trinity, and in a male-dominated Church, Mary is the feminine spirit of God. In the spirit of wisdom, she receives the word in her heart, and brings forth Jesus in his human existence. As a woman, Mary models wisdom in her own faithfulness to living truth and love. She learned to say "Yes" from her life lived in relationship with God, with Joseph, with Jesus, and with all those others whose lives she touched. We are called to that same relationship and singleness of heart so that the gift of God's love living in each of us may come to fullness and be a power of transformation in the world.

Personally, Mary has become friend. She is as near to me in thought and in prayer as was my oldest daughter when as a student she was separated from me by the expanse of the Atlantic Ocean or as other friends and loved ones who are distant in space or time but who share a common life and love and purpose for being. I need others to model life lived in loving response. Mary is one among many, although unique, because she is the mother of Jesus and because in some ways we have grown up together. I have known her for a long time and have rediscovered an old friend after a long absence.

Roslyn and I have shared our reflections with you as a way of inviting you to explore and image Mary with us, and we invite you to continue your reflections in directions meaningful to you.

REFERENCE

Mary G. Durkin, "Rediscovering Mary: An Inspiration for Family Spirituality," *Chicago Studies* 27 (April 1988): 16-37. Excerpt reprinted with permission.

Feast of the Immaculate Conception

Luke 1:26-38

The Annunciation

Yvonne Lucia

Preached at All-School Worship, Colgate Rochester Divinity School/Bexley Hall/Crozer Theological Seminary and Saint Bernard's Institute

Whom I was a child, I went through Catholic grammar school. One of my most vivid memories is of the time we spent in church. On the first Friday of every month, on holy days, during the church's liturgical seasons, we would be bundled up and led single file across a large parking lot from the school into the church. Once inside, it took our eyes a while to adjust to the dim light. The sweet smell of burning beeswax was everywhere. I remember feeling as if I had traveled to a strange, timeless place. I felt surrounded, caught up in awe and mystery. During mass, the hymns sung in Latin, the pungent scent of incense, the light streaming through stained glass filled me with such ecstasy that I almost felt I would burst. To a seven year old, my experience in church was as powerful as Isaiah's vision of the Temple.

But there came a time—I can't remember exactly when—that the beautiful church and those ancient rituals lost their power to evoke a response in me. Piece by piece, the sense of mystery slipped away, like chunks of snow sliding off a roof during a January thaw. And how I long to get back to that time and place where I could taste, touch, and smell the presence of God. How I long to experience that majestic, transcendent, mysterious God that was so tangible to me as a child.

Today, in a similar way, I long for these words of Scripture to come alive again. How I long to hear the beating of angel's wings and to believe that if I looked hard enough, some day I might see one. How I long to look at these words and see them move and breathe, the way that I used to see the baby Jesus move and breathe in the creche at church on Christmas Eve. But somewhere along the way—I can't remember exactly when—these words lost their power to evoke a deep response in myself.

These words of Scripture have become so familiar to us that they no longer stir us as they did when they were fresh for us. And added to our complacency is our shock in learning what the historical-critical method of study has revealed about the Scriptures: that very few "facts" back up what is recorded in the Gospels. Thus, for many of us, a world of meaning that we once knew has fallen apart. And how we long to get it all back together again.

In today's Gospel, Mary's way of looking at the world was shattered, too. The glad tidings brought by the angel did not fit in with her understanding of the way things work. Mary is told that she shall bear a child—but she is a virgin, an unmarried young woman. Mary moves from fear to confusion to transformation as she struggles to understand the angel's message.

And as our own way of looking at the world and at this Scripture is shattered, we too experience fear and confusion. It's so hard to let go of a past which gave meaning and purpose to our lives, to embrace an unknown future. But as Mary moved through fear and confusion to transformation, so must we. We must make these words come alive for ourselves today, here, now—or else they will remain nothing more than the wooden pieces of the creches that we pull out of our attics once a year.

How can we breathe new life into these ancient words? How do they come alive for us again? How can this word become a word of power which calls forth personal response? What is today's story telling us about the truth in our own lives?

Our word today is about salvation coming into the world. God's salvation grows in Mary's womb as the life of one who saves. And this conception of life, this birth of life in the mother's womb, is itself God's saving activity.

God's saving activity is the birth of a child. God's saving activity is the creative and redemptive possibility in the birth of a new life.

Our reading today is about the redemptive impulse of God, ever present in human life. The truth of today's word is this: that salvation is always at work, always giving birth (Song 90-92).

To read the story of the annunciation as a story of redemption is not to take less seriously the incarnation of Jesus. To read the story of the annunciation in this way is to take the incarnation *most* seriously. If birthing, if all of life holds the possibility of salvation, then we are the ones who are asked to give birth to ourselves as the living word of God.

Hear again these old, old words from the Gospel of Luke in a new light:

In the twelfth month of this year, the angel Gabriel was sent from God to this town, with a message for you who are gathered here. The angel went in and said to them, "Greetings, most favored ones. The Lord is with you." But those gathered were troubled by what he said and wondered what his greeting might mean. Then the angel said to them, "Do not be afraid, sisters and brothers, for God has been gracious to you; *you* shall conceive and bear the living Word of God." "How can this be?" they responded, "For we are still learning about God." The angel answered, "The Holy Spirit shall come upon you, and the power of the Most High will overshadow you; and for this reason, the holy child to be born will be called the 'Living Word of God.' Moreover, you will know that all flesh is filled with spirit. The child to be born is yourselves become the Living Word of God."

How will we respond to the angel's annunciation? Will we answer in such a way that a confused and frightened world will be able to hear us when we say, "The Lord, the Living Word is with you?"

Do not be afraid.

REFERENCE

Choan-Seng Song. *The Compassionate God.* Maryknoll: Orbis Books, 1982.

3rd Sunday of Lent (A)

Exodus 17:3-7
Romans 5:1-2,5-8
John 4:5-42

The Samaritan Woman

Kay Heverin, SSJ

Preached for a Dignity/Integrity Community

There are many ways our Scriptures could take us today. Is there anyone among us who could not identify with the grumbling Israelites, complaining that things were better in Egypt when they were slaves than out wandering in the desert? The grumbling came out of their thirst—out of their doubting God's presence, God's promise to care for them always.

When we move to our Gospel, we should have little trouble identifying with the Samaritan woman. You'll remember she chided Jesus for speaking to her—a Samaritan—*and* a woman. Jesus did not associate with Samaritans; men were not to speak to women in public, and to add to it, she was an outcast, needing to come to this well rather than use the one in her village.

We have been seen as outcasts and sinners by some, but we could be called today to reflect on whether we hold any person or group in the same light. Whom do you keep at a distance? Whom do you love? I thought at first I'd go on with this theme, yet I kept coming back to the words of Jesus to the woman "Give me a drink" (Jn 4:7b). Have you been thirsty? Really thirsty? Dying for a drink? What do you thirst for?

We could keep the answers on the surface and say wine, water, scotch, whatever. But the invitation given to the Samaritan woman and to us is to go deeper—risk more.

What do you thirst for? Love, to be special, to have a friend, to belong, to be accepted, to be trusted, to be free to be yourself, to know God?

And once we identify our thirst, are we willing to ask someone for a drink, let someone see us as needy, dependent, or do we insist on saving face, acting as if everything were fine?

Our culture, our society sets up certain barriers. We can pass by each other and never even see the real need or the real person for that matter. Today I believe Jesus is calling us to risk being who we really are. Jesus gives us an example. Instead of hiding his need out of custom, fear, or pride, he came to the woman as he was and in doing so opened up possibilities of new life for her. Jesus would not play a game with her, and so she was free to be herself, to own her sins and her mistakes and move on.

We see from our story that once the Samaritan woman faced herself as she really was, she was free, and we hear that she left her water jar and went back to town to share her good news. She was to become living water for those who had treated her as an outcast.

And what about us? It's fine to read this great story and make a connection to our own life story, but do you really believe and live the way Paul describes in today's reading: "God's love has been poured into our hearts through the Holy Spirit which has been given to us....[W]hile we were yet sinners Christ died for us" (Rom 5:5b, 8b)?

We do not earn or deserve God's love. It simply is God's gift. We have been freed in Christ. Like the woman at the well, do we accept the gift or do we hold ourselves slaves, refuse this freedom—continuing to wander in the wilderness like the Israelites, dying of thirst—bound by fear, self-doubt, worry, selfishness, excuses?

We must discover what keeps us from dipping our bucket into the living water we were given at baptism. What keeps us feeling like a dry, parched, land?

Fullness of life is ours and like the Samaritan woman we are called to be a fountain of life-giving water for others.

"Give me a drink!" What holds us back from responding?

"I don't want to get involved. I've been hurt, used, discarded. I don't have time or energy. I don't have a bucket."

"I'm new here. I'm shy, frightened, unsure. I stand alone."

Give me a drink.

"I'm out of work, in a bad relationship, drinking too much, ill with AIDS."

Give me a drink.

"I'm dishonest, play games, refuse to take responsibility. I need someone to listen. I miss my family. I'm alone."

Give me a drink.

"Give me a drink." So often we miss the request.

So often we refuse to make the request.

"If you knew the gift of God and who it is that is saying to you, 'Give me a drink.'" (Jn 4:10).

We have all we need, in order to respond, to request.

During this Lenten season, we may discover things we must let go of or even things we need to add to life in order to be ready for resurrection.

I'm going to ask you this week to add something: take your bucket, find your well, take time with yourself and ask, what, who refreshes me? Whom do I ask for a drink? After you discover that, then name how you are living water for others. Write it down. Really do it.

We need to look for living water, for fountains in our midst, if we are to accept the free gift of Christ—a gift of living water held out to those with or without bucket, yet a gift that never runs dry.

❁

The Canaanite Woman

Joan Sobala, SSJ

I have always liked the Canaanite woman in today's Gospel, with her quick wit and pungent retorts. But over the years, I keep finding different reasons to turn back to her as a model and mentor for life.

The thing about the Canaanite woman that absorbs me most at the moment is how she kept herself focused on her quest and refused to be sidetracked.

Some commentators point out that the sharp interchange we heard between Jesus and the people was not hostile at all but was really a social skill highly valued in some parts of the world, something like the colorful middle-eastern curse: "May the gnats of ten thousand camels infest your bed."

Reading the dialogue with our western minds, though, we are surprised at Jesus. He is not particularly likable here—apparently demeaning of the woman who is clearly an outsider and holds no claim over Jesus.

In last weekend's Gospel, Jesus may have been able to quiet the advance of the winds and waves, but he was not able to stop this woman's advance.

The woman's attitude was dogged and determined—her prayer the same as water-walking Peter's. "Lord, help me," each of them cried out. "Lord, help me!" (Mt 15:25)

When Jesus tried insult, the woman deftly turned the insult into a compliment, and Jesus was overwhelmed by her powerful faith.

What impresses me most about this woman is how secondary issues did not distract her, however emotionally or rationally compelling these issues were.

She could have walked away in anger because Jesus was treating her in a stereotypical way. She could have taken him on as an arrogant Jew who looked down on Gentile foreigners. Sexist attitudes and racial exclusions are worthy of our combat. But she didn't. She stayed on the point.

It's easy to get sidetracked—as individuals and as communities.

One way the church has gotten sidetracked over the centuries is by putting a great deal of organizational emphasis on clergy who are male and celibate.

We've talked about this topic before, but it's worthwhile seeing it from this perspective. With current clergy dying or leaving and few seminarians in the wings, local communities will have less and less opportunity to be nourished by the Eucharist, which Catholicism has always held to be the center of our life together as well as for our journey.

In this instance, the Canaanite woman is all of us here and throughout the church. We are to be like her, persistently saying to a reluctant authority, "Things are backwards." Do we value the celibate male character of our priests more than we value Eucharist?

That's only one example. In our church and in our world, upholding life values requires that we keep our eye on the donut and not on the hole—and that we stand our ground and speak our piece with creative wit and tenacious trust.

On the other hand, when we as individuals, as a segment of society are approached by those whom we consciously or unconsciously consider inferior, are we willing to learn wisdom from them, to accept their viewpoint and truly listen to and learn from them? The world is divided into the insiders and the outsiders, and the problem is that the insiders define who is in and who is out.

For example, the direction of the church, historically, has been set by European churchmen. They have been the insiders. In our day, the fledgling African church and the emerging Latin American church have brought their cultures and the reflections of their people to the shaping of church life. Our own American church leadership has deliberately set out to listen to the people in the shaping of three pastoral letters.

In general, today's readings all try to get at the same question: Who is important enough to pay attention to? The Gospel has no trouble showing us that inclusiveness in our mentality and practice is hard won.

We are challenged today to have God's own attitude toward humanity: to be welcoming and open, not closed and prohibitive.

So the story of Jesus and the Canaanite woman offers us two questions around which to wrap our thoughts this week: Where do we put our energies? Whom do we welcome?

Along with these questions, the story offers us a prayer to say—as did Peter last week and the Canaanite woman this week—for clarity as we seek answers to these questions: "Lord, help me!" (Mt 15:25).

Luke 13:10-17

The Bent-Over Woman

Sandra Clark Arrington

Preached at Colgate Rochester Divinity School/Bexley Hall/Crozer Theological
Seminary and St. Bernard's Institute

S andra, stand up straight," could easily sum up my life story.
Different voices.
Different times.
Different places.

But for forty plus years—from childhood to mid-life—the words
have echoed in my ears, sometimes spoken as if a command,
"Sandra, stand up straight," sometimes spoken as a gentle reminder,
"Sandra! Stand up *straight.*

In either case, the words seemed to *overpower* me rather than
empower me—as if I could just automatically snap back my
shoulders, hold up my head and look people squarely in the eye—
thereby miraculously transforming my propensity for poor posture.

Recently, though, the refrain "to stand up straight" has taken on a
new sound, a new meaning: it has been transformed into a loving
invitation—to stand erect—to stand tall, as a person who is loved by God!

Is it any wonder that I was drawn to preach on the stooped
woman who for eighteen years had shuffled around, head bowed,
eyes to the ground, her back perhaps bent by the weight of her own
woundedness?

For it is within this Gospel story that the loving invitation—to stand tall, as a person—is offered by Jesus.

Lest this invitation seem like one to RSVP "with regret," let us see what makes the invitation appealing and possible to accept.

Whether she was crippled and handicapped by a birth defect or disease, we will never know, but we do know that the stooped woman was an outcast, most likely ridiculed, shunned, and perhaps even despised because she was a woman and because of her physical appearance. She was a double outcast who very likely bore the crippling wounds of low self-esteem, a poor self-image and a constricted sense of self. Perhaps, the very same words echoed in her ears as they did in mine, only in her case even more hurtfully, "What's wrong with you? Can't you stand up straight?"

And then, one day, Jesus came along, teaching in one of the synagogues along his way to Jerusalem. Jesus' eyes *came to rest* on this lowly, bent-over woman standing apart from the crowd, and he *invited* her to stand tall as a person, to begin to feel good about herself because she *was* accepted and not rejected; she was *loved* and *important* in God's eyes.

"Woman, you are freed from your infirmity" (Lk 13:12b).

Jesus, unlike others, saw her as a human being, a *person*. He treated her as a sister, a friend. He saw who she really was, a daughter of Abraham, a child of God. And he reached out to her, in love, with compassion, with feeling—*person to person*—accepting her, not rejecting her.

But he did even more.

Although she had been a victim of paralysis, crooked, crippled, and dispirited, Jesus, nonetheless, envisioned her as the person she was meant to be, laying hands on her, touching her. The one who was shunned, ridiculed, despised; the one who had known rejection, alienation, and oppression; the one who was weighted down with woundedness felt the life-giving love of God flowing into her and she was nurtured and transformed, empowered to stand erect for the first time in eighteen years!

She was empowered to stand erect for the first time in eighteen years because she finally felt loved and lovable!

And that is the invitation that Jesus extends to all of us today—the invitation to be transformed, the invitation to stand erect, to be released from our bondage of low self-esteem—no matter how unloved or unlovable we feel—*through* the healing and empowering love of God which surpasses all imagination.

The misuses of power are as threatening today as they were in the time of Jesus. But Jesus and his countless followers throughout the ages are witnesses that power can be something other than control, coercion, manipulation, and violence.

For it is through Jesus and such stories as the transformation of the bent-over woman that power takes on a positive image of love and compassion—expressions of power that are nurturing and therefore *empowering*, not overpowering.

Jesus gave us beautiful examples of such power: the miracles, signs of liberating power, and the parables, prophetic judgments about reversal in power relationships: the first, last; the last, first.

We can learn by meditating on the actions of Jesus—perhaps during this Lenten season—that power is intended to mediate God's love within the human community. We can learn that the power of which Jesus speaks is a power which transforms both the individual and the community.

This is an important message for us to reflect on, for it is the nurturing power of God which energizes and gives us hope in the face of the evils which exist in our world today.

But how easy it is to forget that the nurturing power of God is more effective than the power of evil—until we are reminded by the story of the bent-over woman. Although she was an outcast by gender and bodily form, God took the initiative and reached out to this marginalized woman with empowering love so that she could be set free—attesting to God's power and presence in the midst of suffering caused by evil in the world.

This stooped woman, who had shuffled around for so many years with her eyes to the ground, was very likely *resigned* to her fate, knowing it was not "her place" to *complain* or *attain*. Believing her condition was somehow her fault, she shuffled around with her head low, her eyes to the ground, her shoulders stooped because she felt unloved and unworthy—the wounds of rejection weighing her down.

And then it happened. The great mystery of God's love for each person finally broke through, cutting through all resistance, all barriers, including the power of the satanic, so that this lowly, suffering woman could be set free, to be.

God's love is unlike any other love because it is so healing and nurturing that it has the power to radically transform. Even the most broken and wounded can become a new creation.

But let us look at this new creation, this daughter of Abraham, now standing erect in the midst of the assembly.

Clearly, this woman had been changed and transformed by God. Radiant and full of life—the power and presence of God so real that there was no self-doubt, no propensity to return to her former self.

But what happened to this woman over time? If we subscribe to healing being a process, then this woman would have been like the rest of us—continually experiencing the tension between "the already" and the "not yet."

She knew that God loved her and she experienced that love. Yet she struggled to live out of that love in a world which led her to believe she was inferior and unworthy.

For no matter how transforming God's love is, we still struggle to feel good about ourselves. We struggle to believe that we are loved and lovable.

On one hand, we believe that God loves us, that we are created in God's image and likeness, that we are good, precious in God's eyes and even God's artwork. On the other hand, we struggle to integrate these affirmations into our self-concept.

Why is this so hard for us to internalize, to believe with all our hearts and souls and minds to such an extent that we can truly live out of this wellspring of God's love for each of us?

Basically, it is the messages so received over the years which when internalized as "not being lovable" constrict us and restrict us. They cause us to resist God's free and gracious gift of unconditional love, time and time again; they block our ability to love ourselves and to accept love from others. Removed from the nurturing power of love, these messages severely constrict and restrict us from our God-given potential.

These messages come from many sources. Our parents, authority figures, the media, social evils, sexism, racism, and classism are a few. They can tear us apart and cut us to the quick. And they subtly erode our self-esteem and self-concept over time.

The nurturing power of love can not be overestimated. Without it, people can wither and die or become crippled, paralyzed like the bent-over woman.

Years ago in well-known laboratory experiments, baby monkeys languished when fed mechanically from a twisted, cold wire figure. But they prospered when comforted by a softly pillowed form. It does not take much to imagine the devastating effects on humans deprived of love.

We know that people have survived the most inhumane
conditions. Such a thought brings to mind the description of Nelson
Mandela upon being released from prison after twenty-seven-and-
a-half years. After solitary confinement, back-breaking work, illness
and promises of freedom if he would only compromise his ideals, he
emerged smiling, almost shyly, with no apparent bitterness.

The description went something like this: "Mandela's voice
sounded firm, his words eloquent. Though he looked all of his
seventy-one years and was greyer than artists' renditions over the
years, he walked out of Victor Verster prison *erect and tall.*"

It was not surprising to later read that Mandela was a person
nurtured and sustained by love. For the tender love letters he wrote
his wife, Winnie, from prison had become an issue when included
in a recent biography. His former law partner asked to have them
removed from the book because he thought it wasn't dignified for a
man of Mandela's stature. but Mandela overruled the request,
saying words to this effect: "You leave it all in. It's true. There's no
reason to hide these things."

Such a story is inspiring because it helps us to see how very
resilient humans are if sustained by love. And such a story draws us
back into the story of the bent-over woman.

Remember, we left her empowered by God's love: standing
erect, radiant, and full of life—and yet realizing that the moment of
radical transformation was the *beginning* of a healing process. Faced
with the hardships of her day, faced with being a woman in a man's
world, what would happen to her over time? Could she remain erect
and tall—now able to be nurtured by the wellspring of God's love—
even if she were to experience no other love?

Stories such as Nelson Mandela's say standing tall is possible.
We also find our hope and assurance in the fact that Jesus released
the woman from bondage on the sabbath. The assurance unfolds
like this:

> Raised by Jesus on the sabbath
>
> in an obscure house of worship
>
> in an unnamed town,
>
> an anonymous woman
>
> becomes a sign of God's reign.

The sabbath was *the* appropriate day to have the nurturing power of God's love break through for this marginalized daughter of Abraham for the sabbath is symbolic of God's outreach to humankind.

The sabbath is the climax of God's *creative* activity and a day of special blessing for God's people.

The purpose of the sabbath is to protect humans from exploitation.

In stretching straight up, the woman became a sign that a new order prevailed—initiated by Jesus as the one who walks with us. Jesus empowers us to transform ourselves and our broken world. Is it any wonder that in stretching straight up this daughter of Abraham praised God?

The Adulterous Woman: Gettin' a Twenty-Second Chance

Toinette M. Eugene

Day after day, week after week, the American public has been treated to a detailed media account of more than we would ever want to know about the lurid life and times of Robert Packwood, U.S. Senator. His story makes you want to give up reading the newspaper.

But then there was another poignant soap opera serial that caught my eye recently. The front page article headlined "Tiffany and Tashonda Reunited." The story recounted the happy ending of a story sequel—a young unmarried black teenager who had reported that she and her sister found a newborn in the trash and had given it to social service for foster care.

The reader subsequently learns that Tiffany had actually given birth to the child herself but was too afraid and too unprepared to care for it. The judge, who at his first ruling, had refused to return the child to its mother, offered a second chance. Somehow, he had developed a new outlook on those two lives and had a new legal opinion that brought a judgment of wholeness, and reconciliation. Some might even call it merciful forgiveness in the case of this apparently errant teenager. Or better yet, it might be described as the age-old dispensation of what my grandmother calls, "Gettin' a twenty-second chance."

I am preaching from these newspaper stories because reading the news is one surefire way I have learned to know God. I believe that prayer is made much more real when I pray with the New Testament in one hand and the newspaper in the other. And this weekend, I am struck by the similarities between the story we have heard proclaimed in the Gospel and the unhappy contemporary stories which I stumble over and struggle with in *Time* magazine or the *New York Times*.

I know what I think about Robert Packwood and the evidence offered about his apparent sexual misconduct and inappropriateness as a public official. I know how I feel in reading about the reunion of Tiffany and Tashonda, my younger sisters, my family in a sense, by faith and by African-American cultural tradition. What do these parables and people teach me and tell me in relation to the sacred story of Jesus and the woman who is most often referred to as "the woman taken in adultery"? How shall I pray and change and grow in relation to these very present parables of human life and God's ongoing action of grace in our midst?

The encounter between Jesus and the Pharisees debating over the fate of an adulteress is not found in some of the earliest traditions of the New Testament, or at least it has no fixed place in our ancient witnesses. But no apology is needed for this once-independent story which has found its way into the fourth Gospel and some manuscripts in Luke. The first reason that this fragment remained in the memories of those who handed on the traditions was because it recalls the image and posture of Jesus as a forgiving, tender, and compassionate Lord.

Its succinct expression of the mercy of Jesus is as delicate as anything in Luke; its portrayal of Jesus as the serene judge has all the majesty that we would expect of John. The moment when the sinful woman stands confronted with the sinless Jesus is one of exquisite drama. When the woman's accusers heard what Jesus said, they went away one by one. He was left alone with the woman still there before him.

The delicate balance between the justice of Jesus in not condoning the sin and his mercy in forgiving the sinner is one of the great lessons of the Gospel. Robert Packwood and Tiffany Anderson are not alone. We have been there also and not only once.

A second reason that the story remains as a canonical text even though its authorship is unclear is that its point is akin to that of other scenes in which the attitude of Jesus toward women is being questioned. His attitude was challenged not only by his contemporary enemies but also by moralists within the early church who retained the memory of this episode. This unique story brings with it a distinctive note, for it deals not only with a legal question but also with a sensitive sexual ethics issue.

On the surface, the accusers of the woman are right. The cards seem hopelessly stacked against the adulterous woman. This woman, who is forced to stand before Jesus and all the people in the Temple area, has been caught, they triumphantly and publicly announce, "in adultery" (Jn 8:3b). She is not only apprehended in the criminal act, but the law clearly states that "both the adulterer and the adulteress shall be put to death" since it was a capital offense against the woman's husband. Here, neither the husband nor the lover is mentioned. This is obviously sexism.

Jesus knows that the strict religionists, the canon lawyers, and others who brought the woman to him, were attempting to entrap him. If Jesus upheld the law and recommended stoning the woman, he would get into trouble with the Roman authorities since the Jewish court was not permitted to carry out capital punishment. But if he showed mercy, he would be flagrantly flouting the most sacred Jewish traditions.

But Jesus lifts the case from the level of legal discussion to that of psychological analysis. He focuses not on the character of the guilty woman but on her male accusers' self awareness and true motivation. This shift enabled Jesus to introduce the theological issue of *social* sinfulness in contrast to illegal acts that might be catalogued as *individual* and *private* sins. The distinction was evidently not familiar to his audience.

What is the distinction Jesus is making? What about the situation that brought the woman before Jesus? Sexual irregularity, infringement of a right, affront to a man's honor, violation of the mores of a particular society, a breach of ethics? Jesus did not for a moment deny this reality, but instead he placed a distinctly sinful woman in the larger context of sinful humanity.

This woman belonged equally in the same category as that of men who were seemingly perfect and scrupulously observant of the law. For Jesus, legal righteousness could not be isolated from innate oneness with the human family. He affirmed the solidarity of the human race, both in our propensity to sin as well as in our equality in dignity and in personhood before God. One cannot really condemn the sexual irregularities of others without placing them in the larger context of social injustice and double standards. Jesus, however, chose to say something both supportive and salvific about the injustice which women and other minorities have endured at the hands of those who control the legal and social systems.

The woman was prostrate on the ground. Society had abased her into shame. She had lost her dignity, her self-respect. She was in dread of losing her life. Jesus seemed about to agree with her accusers, but his judgment instead brought out a basic affirmation of our equality before the law and especially before God. "Let him who is without sin among you be the first to throw a stone at her" (Jn 8:7b). Then a true miracle happened. The virtuous men departed, one by one!

The comment of the narrator of this New Testament fragment shrewdly discloses the attitude of Jesus. His exquisite care and fairness toward all human beings, men or women, transcends inherited prejudices, the pull of custom, and even the dictates of the law that was deemed to be divinely ordained.

Jesus did not condemn the woman, but he added, "Go and do not sin again" (Jn 8:11b). The woman was restored to wholeness, to grace, and given what we all hunger for: a "twenty-second chance."

Her response, which we do not have recorded, is traditionally depicted as that of profound thanksgiving for God's gracious forgiveness.

What is our response to these stories? What have we gained, observed, learned, from reading about Robert Packwood and Tiffany Anderson, and the passage on the adulterous woman which has been traditionally located in the Gospel of John? What have these lessons offered for my Easter preparation, for my life in these days yet to come?

In joining the contemporary news to the Good News, the lesson seems transparent and piercingly plain as manifested in the action and words of Jesus offered to the woman, to the religious leaders, and to us:

- The lesson is that when asked to give judgment,
  Jesus says we must first judge ourselves.

- The lesson is not that I should deny being a Pharisee. I shall always be hypocritical and judgmental. This fact I know well, to my discomfort and shame.

- The lesson is not to overlook my own forms of unfaithfulness to promises and commitments or the sloppiness in my loving.

- *The lesson is*, nonetheless, an invitation to be unconditionally forgiving, tender, and compassionate as Jesus is—forgetful of the past and hopeful for the future in which no one's freedom is abused and in which dignity is restored.

Luke 10:38-42
John 11:1-27

My Sister: A Reflection
on Luke 10:38-42 and John 11:1-27

Theresa Stanley

Martha, Martha,
You are busy about many things,
Ageless woman of Bethany,
And in that activity is
  Presence
    and
  Purpose.

You have come to be known to us,
  as active woman,
  engaged in worthless worrying,
  fussing and fretting,
    over
  daily chores.

As one who has chosen
  the part
  less good.

But are you more than this?

The Scriptures say:

You, Martha, are minister
Initiator
Risk-taker,
Warmly welcoming the stranger, who once was the Lord.

You, woman of Menial Work,
are also,
Oganizer
Facilitator
Reflective sister,
The first to recognize the Lord, as Giver of Life.

After Lazarus' death,
leaving house and friends,
you run to meet the Lord,

alone,

decisively and assertively...
breaking the accepted conventions of your culture,
fearlessly expressing grief, anger, disappointment,
daring to honestly share, how He had let you down:

"If you had been here, my brother would not have died"
(Jn 11:21b).

Your certitude—God will give you what you ask (Jn 11:22)—
calls forth
the
Life-Giver...

You, Martha,
intuitively recognize the Lord, the Giver of Life,
even before,
He reveals
Himself.

You, Martha, become the first, to experience
Jesus as Resurrection,
Long before, Easter morn,
even before your brother's rising.[1]

As passionate as Peter, the rock and foundation,
You profess your faith:

"You are the Christ, the son of God, he who is coming into the
world" (Jn 11:27).

Yet, your profession of faith,
  is not revered and remembered,
  as that of Peter.

It has been discounted,
  busy woman,
of Bethany's many things.

On this day, and in this place,
  Martha,
    beloved sister,
    loved one of the Lord,
    woman of deep faith and action,

I reclaim you, and your faith's profession.

For you are my sister,
  busy as I,
Yet recognizing the Life-Giver in the midst of your activity.

Help us to do the same.

Note

1. The concept in this and the preceding verse is based on an idea presented
   by Elisabeth Moltmann-Wendel, *The Women Around Jesus* (New York:
   Crossroad, 1982), 26.

Martha

Roni Antenucci

Preached at All-School Worship, Colgate Rochester Divinity School/Bexley Hall/Crozer Theological Seminary and St. Bernard's Institute

M artha, Martha, you are worried and distracted by many things" (Lk 10:41b).

I keep hearing those words over and over again in my head.

Of course I'm distracted by many things. Does Jesus think that food will just appear magically on the table when he's finished his teaching? Does he think his words will fill hungry stomachs? It wouldn't be so bad if he just came by himself; then I wouldn't have to fuss so. But he never comes alone. He always has those friends with him. And it's not as though I'm making a feast. But they do need to eat.

Sure, I'd like to sit and listen to him, too, sometimes. And just once, it would be nice if Mary *offered* to help in the kitchen. I'm tired of always being the one responsible for seeing that our guests' needs are taken care of; yet the reality is I'm better at it then Mary is. Even when she does help, she isn't very good in the kitchen. I know how hard it is for her to clean and bake and cook. She always seems to have her mind on other things. She kind of has her head in the clouds. You see, she has this burning desire to learn about things and is desperate to discuss the Torah with Jesus and other people.

Doesn't she know that we're only women and that women have no business discussing Scripture? Why, I can't tell you how many times I've heard my brother, Lazarus, pray, "Thank you, God, that I am not a Gentile. Thank you, God, that you did not make me a woman or ignorant."

All my life I've seen and heard men study and discuss the Scriptures, and there have been so many times when I wanted to sit among them. But I've been taught that it's not for me to do. My place is in the kitchen, isn't it?

But Mary's out there, sitting at the rabbi's feet; and he told me that she has chosen the better part. I just don't understand. What does he mean by that?

You know, one of the things that I love about Jesus is the way that he takes me so seriously, as if everything I have to say is important. He often stops here on his way to Jerusalem, and he's never spoken to me like this before. It's just not like him. "The better part, the better part..." (Lk 10:42). What can he mean? He can't really mean that serving others isn't important because he does it himself. Why, it wasn't long ago that he fed a huge crowd who came to hear his words. Some said that there were more than five thousand people there. So he knows how important it is to serve others. I mean, there are meals to be made, clothing to be sewn, the house to be cleaned, and people to be cared for. Someone has to do it. And it won't get done around here if I become like Mary and drop everything to sit at Jesus' feet to listen to his words.

Besides, if I'm really honest, I'm good at doing things for others, and I like to do them. Why, it would be just as hard for me to sit still and listen and learn as it would be for Mary to organize and run the household. Though I have to admit it, hard as it is for her, she sometimes does it. Not very well, but she does it.

Is that it?

I know that sometimes I want nothing more than to be in Jesus' presence, to soak in all he has to tell me; but I always have so much to do, and I just don't often find the time to reflect on Jesus' words. Is he scolding me? Or is he inviting me to be his disciple, too?

Why is it so hard for me to quiet myself? Am I too comfortable with my busyness? Has it become a compulsion for me? Maybe Mary chose the better part because she listened to the voice within her, because she accepted the words of life Jesus had to give her.

I think perhaps my sister's call is sometimes different than mine. I guess I've judged her pretty harshly. But does that mean that action is less important than contemplation? Somehow I don't think so. Certainly, Jesus knows that both are necessary; and I'm coming to see both in my life.

Maybe Jesus is saying that Mary chose the better part because she listened to the voice of God within her and responded to God's call to sit at the feet of Jesus today. I don't think I was asked to sit at Jesus' feet today just as Mary wasn't asked to serve today. But the next time Jesus stops by on his travels, we might each be called to do the things that are more difficult for us. Mary would be called to action; what a cross that would be for her. I might be called to sit at the rabbi's feet, silent and still. Why, for me that would be the hardest thing, a heavy cross to bear.

My need for action is sometimes a compulsion, and Mary's need for stillness and contemplation can be that, too. To choose the better part, we may both be called to embrace our crosses—to do the thing that's hardest.

How about you? What is your compulsion? What is the cross you may need to embrace to choose the better part?

Mary and Elizabeth

Deni Mack

Both Mary and Elizabeth were unlikely mothers—Mary because she was not married and Elizabeth because she was old. But nothing is impossible with God. In today's Gospel story, we see Mary running to Elizabeth. Mary didn't go only to help Elizabeth; Mary also needed support. Mary was in trouble. Just ten lines before this story, the Gospel writer Luke says, "she was greatly troubled" (Lk 1:29a). The pictures and statues we have of Mary show her as serene. But Mary *was* troubled and needed Elizabeth's understanding, compassion, and support. And she got it. An unwed, pregnant teenager welcomed the warm space of wise-old-woman hugging. Each became her sister's keeper as expressing tears and fears was as safe as expressing joy. Two women came to discover what God was doing in their lives. Graced by God and by each other, Elizabeth not only welcomed Mary but also recognized that her cousin carried her Lord in her womb, and she *received* Mary into her home.

We are so busy doing things that we need a change of mind to *receive* whatever concerns others bring to us. We're so busy solving problems that a deep change of heart is required for us to *receive*. It is one thing to have a party or a meeting and welcome people; it is something deeper to recognize that this person carries Christ into my home, into this meeting, into this church, and into the shop where I'm finding one last Christmas gift. When we're too full of our own agendas, there's no room in our hearts to really *receive* people.

While it is beautiful to picture Mary and Elizabeth, a young girl and her aged relative, both pregnant with new life, it is even more beautiful for each of us to recognize that we are each pregnant with God's life. That is why God made us—to bring to life all that God has placed within us; that's how we give honor and glory to God. That is what happened in our baptism, when the community celebrated that we belong to God's family, a family formed to bring to birth all that is of God in each one of us and to help each one of us to be our unique expression of carrying Jesus, birthing Jesus, and recognizing Jesus.

We say the "Hail Mary," the prayer begun in today's Gospel, and hear incredible discovery. Imagine Elizabeth's face as she says, "Blessed are you among women, and blessed is the fruit of your womb!" (Lk 1:42). The honor of carrying Jesus, while uniquely Mary's, is also ours. Each of us carries Jesus; each of us is in labor to give birth to Jesus. We can even feel Jesus—especially in the Eucharist. And we are blessed by Jesus at all times. Maybe we don't stop and acknowledge his deep abiding presence until we realize that Jesus is present to us just as Mary and Elizabeth realized.

Here is an instance of an ordinary person carrying Jesus and of her baby leaping for joy: Barbara and her son, Darren, had a difficult morning. Maybe thirteen-month-old Darren had an earache or was teething; he had wakened his parents up often throughout the night, and he was cranky all morning. When Barbara put him down for a nap, she thought, "Thank God for naps. Oh, God, help Darren to sleep. I need a break from this whining child." Two blessed hours later, Barbara heard Darren singing, an invitation to change his diaper and start round two. As Barbara opened the bedroom door, Darren greeted her by bouncing up and down and squealing with delight. Barbara said, "I had never before been greeted with such enthusiasm"—something like the way Elizabeth and her leaping baby greeted Mary. Barbara deserves such a greeting as she carries Jesus to Darren. And Darren's spontaneous joy builds Barbara's confidence; she's ready to tackle round two of baby care.

Elizabeth's baby John leapt for joy in her womb at the approach of his cousin Jesus in Mary's womb. When our hearts leap for joy or compassion, that's a sign of God's presence.

Maybe no one's heart leaps when we walk into a room, but we need affirmation. We don't have Elizabeth to tell us "blessed is our fruit," and we don't have baby Darren to squeal with joy at us. So we need people at work to support and encourage us. And we may not find them there. We need a relative or friend to give us a word of acknowledgment; we form support groups in which each one's presence is a blessing to the group. Yet some receive no greeting until a stranger thanks them for holding a door or a salesperson looks into their eyes and says, "Keep warm; blessed Christmas," or a volunteer gives them a warm bed in a shelter.

More important than our need for welcome and appreciation is our need to be like Elizabeth ourselves and recognize the presence of Christ in one another. We need to *give* people encouragement. God puts people in our paths, and we don't even notice that they're pregnant with Christ.

When we allow God to do the impossible with us, we create a space for the Mary's in our lives to carry Jesus to us. Mary and Elizabeth opened their hearts to God and discovered that God could do the impossible. Each moment of our lives is pregnant with possibilities. Right in the imperfections and frustrations of our ordinary day, God makes us pregnant with hope, pregnant with love, and pregnant with Christ even when we find ourselves as barren as old, childless Elizabeth. Maybe our feeling of being barren comes with a job to do at home, school, or work that we feel—no way can we do it. We turn to God as Mary did and as Elizabeth did, and grace comes: a friend helps, or a question is answered; a manual is read; an insight is shared, and all of a sudden the wheels start to turn, and yes, we find that we can do it. We discover that we are pregnant with possibilities. God sees to that.

Yet there are still barren places in us, places where we have said, "Oh, counseling will never save this marriage" or, "I'll never find a job" or "Who, me teach religion?" It's our barrenness that says, "I can't help the homeless" or "This addiction has me hooked." We are barren. But with God, nothing is impossible. If we believe, like Mary, that Jesus was planted into this world in us, if we believe in Jesus' promise, then we work and pray through doubts and hurts, and, yes, we do believe. That belief empowers us to be something like Elizabeth and a little like Mary. We can encourage each other, and goodness will grow, and *he will be born*. God impregnates us with Jesus so that we can carry Jesus to one another, so that we can recognize Christ in one another. Blessed are we who believe that God's promises will be fulfilled.

The Unnamed Woman
of Mark 14:3-9:
Mary, Mary, Quite the Contrary!

Roslyn A. Karaban

The passage just read would seem to be about a woman who performs a significant and memorable act. It is such a significant act that Jesus proclaims, "What she has done will be told in memory of her" (Mk 14:9b). The act itself has been remembered throughout the ages "wherever the gospel is preached in the world" (Mk 14:9a). And yet the woman who performs this act does not enjoy this same fame. Not only is she unnamed, but when she is named, it seems to be a case of mistaken identity. Today, we will look more closely at this act and in particular what we know about the woman who performed this memorable deed.

The anointing story appears in all four Gospels. In the Gospels of Mark and Matthew (Mt 26:6-13), the anointing is part of the passion narrative but has been given a different setting and place in John (Jn 12:1-8). In the Gospel of Luke (Lk 7:36-38ff), the anointing is related to Jesus' Galilean ministry. Many biblical scholars believe that Mark's account of the anointing story probably comes closest to what the first form of this story must have been; it is Mark's version that was probably used by the authors of the

Gospels of Matthew, Luke, and John. Therefore, it would seem that we would pay special attention to Mark's account.

The Act

As Mark tells the story, Jesus was at Bethany in the house of Simon the leper. A woman, whose name and position are unrecorded, comes with an alabaster flask of ointment of pure nard, an apparently costly aromatic oil worth three hundred denarii, believed to be three hundred days wages—almost a year's work. She breaks the flask and pours oil over Jesus' head.

Some people at the home, who in the Gospel of Mark also remain unnamed, question the act and reproach the woman. Jesus, however, speaks up in defense of the woman and recognizes her action as an expression of an honor due to him, as a spontaneous act of love and devotion, and he accepts the act as such. He even goes so far as to scold those who have criticized the woman, saying, "For you always have the poor with you, and whenever you will, you can do good to them; but you will not always have me" (Mk 14:7). Mark also adds an eschatological consideration (Mk 14:8): the woman's anointing serves as an embalming for Jesus' upcoming burial since in Mark's version of Jesus' death there is no proper anointing of the body. The woman's anointing, therefore, becomes an anticipatory embalming.

The anointing has also been interpreted to have other meanings, including a recognition on the part of the woman of Jesus' royal dignity. This interpretation would be in keeping with what we know from the Hebrew Scriptures (Old Testament) that the head of a king was anointed in recognition of his royal status. On the other hand, we may be reading too much into the significance of this anointing, and the anointing may be no more than the courteous anointing of an honored dinner guest.

According to the Gospel of Mark, Jesus makes one final remark with regard to this unnamed woman: "And truly, I say to you, wherever the gospel is preached in the whole world, what she has done will be told in memory of her" (Mk 14:9). This third remark of Jesus marks the act as of extraordinary value, something worth remembering always. This remark is included in the Gospels of Matthew and Mark, but the Gospels of Luke and John have left it out. This remark, particularly the first part, may be a later addition to the story, an instruction about the importance of proclaiming the good news to the whole world. However, whether this part of the remark is a later addition or not, this action of the woman is the only action in any of the Gospels that is promised a lasting memory, to be recounted for generations to come. We may conclude, then, that this act, recorded in some form in all four Gospels, made a profound impression on those who witnessed it. And yet, what do we know about the woman who performed this act?

The Woman: Mary, Mary, Quite the Contrary!

The author of the Gospel of Mark tells us nothing about the woman—not her name, nor her status, whether she was married or unmarried, young or old, or even what she was doing at the house. Nor does the author of the Gospel of Matthew reveal any information about the woman. We must look to the Gospels of Luke and John to get information about the woman; in doing so, however, we find that these Gospels make significant changes in the story and in the identity of the woman.

The Gospel of John places the anointing story in the village of Bethany, a village often identified with Lazarus and his sisters Martha and Mary. In the Gospel of John, Jesus is at the home of Mary, Martha, and Lazarus, and it is *Mary* who anoints the *feet* of Jesus and wipes his feet with her hair.

In the Gospel of Luke (Lk 7:37), the woman is identified as a *sinful* woman, a woman of the city, in other words a *prostitute*, whose tears fall on Jesus' feet; she wipes them with her hair, kisses his feet, and anoints his feet with oil. In the Gospel of Luke, Jesus also forgives the woman's sins.

It is Luke's version which leaves an impression on our minds, and we are used to reading the Markan version in light of Luke and remembering and identifying the unnamed woman of Mark with a *sinful* woman even though Mark does not say this (Fiorenza xiv).

In the fourth century, the identity of Mark's unnamed woman took another turn. The Syrian Church father Ephraem identified the woman of Mark's story with Mary Magdalene, pointing out that later in the Gospel of Mark (Mk 15:40), Mary Magdalene appears (again). Ephraem also links the sinful woman of Luke 7:37 with Mary Magdalene, and this connection has remained with us today. Mary Magdalene has become known as a classic example of the penitent sinner—in relation to Luke's anointing story. However, the woman of Mark's anointing story is *not* named, and there is really *no* basis for identifying her with Mary Magdalene. The title of this homily, "Mary, Mary, Quite the Contrary!" is taken from a children's nursery rhyme entitled, "Mary, Mary, Quite Contrary." The Mary of the nursery rhyme title refers to Mary, Queen of Scots (sixteenth century), whose lively manners and way of ruling were quite *contrary* to what the famous Puritan Church leader John Knox preached. My title is used to explain that although the Gospel of John has identified the unnamed woman of Mark with Mary of Bethany, Mary #1, and although the church father Ephraem identified this unnamed woman with Mary Magdalene, Mary #2, careful exegesis reveals that the unnamed woman is unlikely to have been either of these two Marys: Mary, Mary, Quite the Contrary!

The Woman and the Act Today

In today's exploration, we have seen that a story which is retold can take on many different versions, and the original story may become blurred. We have also seen that the identity and act of a woman can be changed, and tradition contributes to that change.

Unfortunately, this type of alteration in relation to women occurs all too often in our interpretations of Bible passages.

In the story we just looked at, Mark's version seems the most likely version for a number of reasons, and yet this version underwent significant changes, some of which are quite damaging to the woman and to women in general. Elisabeth Schussler Fiorenza concludes that it is probable that in the original version of the story it was a *woman* who anointed Jesus' *head* and that this was understood as a prophetic recognition of Jesus as the Messiah, the Christ. This would mean, then, that it was a *woman* who first named Jesus as Messiah by her prophetic action. This would be a politically *dangerous* story and would, therefore, be likely to undergo some changes (Fiorenza xiv).

In this regard, we might ask why it is that in Mark's Gospel, while three disciples figure prominently (Peter, Judas, and the unnamed woman who anoints Jesus), only the names of Peter, who denies Jesus, and Judas, who betrays Jesus, are remembered while the name of the woman, who by her action proves herself to be a faithful, devoted disciple, is entirely lost to us.

Because of these sorts of alterations and misinterpretations of stories, some feminists would say that Christian women cannot and should not accept the Bible as their Scripture. For them, the Bible is just too androcentric, too male-centered, too patriarchal, and too sexist to speak to women. Some also claim that Jesus, a male savior, cannot be a model for women. This is one possible reaction to this awareness that certain biblical texts have indeed been distorted, and this view needs to be considered. However, there are other possible reactions to approaching the Bible in light of our knowledge that the Bible is the product of a male-dominated society and therefore predominantly male-oriented. This homily suggests one other approach.

There are some Christian feminists, myself included, who are not willing to totally throw away Scripture. However, we are committed to *reconstructing* early Christian history as *women's* history as well as men's history, as *herstory* as well as *hisstory*. This reconstruction takes the form of 1) *restoration*—restoring women's stories to early Christian history—as well as 2) *reclamation*—reclaiming early Christian history as the history of women and men (Fiorenza xiv).

This approach does not *deny* the presence of androcentrism in the texts nor the maleness of Jesus but looks beyond this to the *content* and *meaning* of the Gospel message. Jesus was not only male, nor did he only represent males, but he represents the new *person*. He came to redeem the *whole* of human nature, male *and* female.

If we look at *who* Jesus associated with, we most often see him with the poor and oppressed, the outcast and sinner, men and women alike. And Jesus came to liberate those oppressed.

Whatever we know or understand about the unnamed woman of Mark's anointing story should be considered in relation to Jesus' reaction and reply to her. He does not rebuke her for what she does, but he instead speaks out against the crowd's reaction, supports her, uplifts her action, and singles it out as an extraordinary act to be remembered as long as the story is told.

This homily has suggested that our contemporary experiences of and attitudes toward women encourage us to approach scriptural stories with different questions and different expectations. In reading Mark's story today, we wonder *why* this woman wasn't named, *who* she was, and *what* might have happened to her. Our new understandings may help us to better respond to women and men who feel alienated, alone, unaccepted, misunderstood, or searching for identity in church and society. We will hopefully look beyond the individual experiences of pain to the systems of oppression (such as patriarchy) that are causing or contributing to this pain.

And we will be empowered to do this because of our new understandings of such passages as Mark 14:3-9, which teaches us that what Jesus came to do for all people is:

- to reach out to and support the oppressed,

- to speak out against the status quo,

- to identify, uphold and lift up acts of noble intention, courage, and love of women and men,

- to point our attention to these acts as sources of empowerment for people in their struggling, and

- to do all these things through his actions and the spreading of his word.

This is what Jesus came to do—for all women and men. May we always keep this in our memory.

REFERENCE

Fiorenza, Elisabeth Schüssler. *In Memory of Her: A Feminist Theological Reconstruction of Christian Origins.* London: SCM Press, 1983.

PART 3

Uplifting the Women of Today: Celebrating Our Gifts

Ruth 1:8-18
Luke 13:10-17

Celebrating the Gifts of Women: Women's Sunday

Barbara Moore, RSM

Preached at First Presbyterian Church, Pittsford, New York

Almost two weeks ago, I attended the funeral of a friend of mine. We had met often in the county jail, and she was a special person. I cannot forget her. At her funeral service, as the priest lifted the bread and said the words of blessing, "This is my body broken for you," I was profoundly moved because her body had been broken by violence, drugs, prostitution, and now murder.

Two thousand years ago, another woman, broken in body because of a crippling disease, isolated by custom and perhaps linked to sin because of cultural misunderstandings, also heard powerful words. "Woman, you are freed from your infirmity" (Lk 13:12b). At once, Luke tells us "she was made straight and she praised God" (Lk 13:13b).

Those who knew my friend, June, could see her potential, her delightful personality, her ability to lead, and could testify to the influence she had on the other women in the jail. Those who knew the bent-over woman could testify to her eighteen years of suffering and yet her deep faith. That faith drew her again and again to the synagogue to pray.

I wish there could have been such a direct and dramatic miracle in June's life. I wish God could have reached out and touched *her* in such a visible way so that as a "free woman" she could have stood straight in the love of her God. Yet even as I share these words, I hesitate because how do I know the ways in which and through whom God touched her and the ways in which she praised that presence...ways only God knows?

The synagogue officials of Luke's Gospel wanted to dismiss the miracle and focus on Jesus' attitude toward the sabbath tradition. The fact that the woman could stand straight and that she praised God meant little to them. What mattered to them was that Jesus had broken the law.

Two women, lifestyle for one, and illness for another, placed them at odds with their communities.

Two women also appear in our Hebrew Scriptures this morning: Naomi and her daughter-in-law Ruth. Naomi had lost not only her husband but two sons as well. She was totally dependent upon her tribal roots and the male members of her family. Naomi was determined to return to her home in Bethlehem and seek the help that so many dependent widows sorely needed. Her foreign daughters-in-law were supposed to do the same because of the death of their spouses. But Ruth, in a deeply moving passage, rejected the prescribed customs of the day and said to Naomi, "Entreat me not to leave you or return from following you; for where you go I will go and where you lodge I will lodge" (Ruth 1:16).

The women of today's Scriptures, Naomi, Ruth, and the bent-over woman, were victims of the culture of their day, a culture that held them within a structure that contained rigid socio-economic norms, a culture that laid out for them prescribed roles and expectations. These roles and expectations often left women in positions of dependence, weakness, and inferiority. The beauty of Ruth's story is her willingness to rise above expectations and respond to the needs of Naomi. As a result of this loving and brave action, new life awaited both of them. The Scriptures tell us that Ruth remarried and from that union came a son who would be the ancestor of King David. And from David's line came Jesus the Christ.

So, too, the Lord rose above cultural expectations. Think of the boldness of Jesus as he took the initiative to speak to a woman in public, for this was a forbidden action. He actually touched her and risked ritual impurity. Rachel Conrad Wahlberg, in her book *Jesus and the Freed Woman*, shares this insight: the story of the freed woman has been unfortunately overlooked, and rarely preached on, despite its powerful witness to Jesus' ministry and to his attitude toward women (17).

Yet this story reveals the Jesus we have come to know and love. His embrace was for all. It crossed cultural, gender, and traditional lines and reached out to those in need. "You hypocrites!...And ought not this woman, a daughter of Abraham, whom Satan bound for eighteen years, be loosed from this bond on the sabbath day?" (Lk 13:15a,16).

Many women, both within the church and the wider community, are bound by cultural, social, and theological bonds that must be loosened. The Junes whom I have met in the jail, for example, suffer from profoundly low self-esteem and often are seeking their identities outside themselves. As many of them search for that identity, they become involved with the criminal justice system.

Those bonds are also present within our church. Some of the bonds are very subtle, and we women fall into expected patterns of behavior. But in some denominations, such as my own, the bonds are quite clear. Many of us who have felt them in both subtle and apparent ways find them not only painful but sinful.

We within the church, both men and women, have much work ahead of us as we try to erase some of the destructive misunderstandings that date back to the theological giants of the early and medieval church. Whether or not we realize it, these misunderstandings are alive and well within our Churches. They are misunderstandings that place women in structured positions of inferiority. They are misunderstandings that question whether we, as women, are made fully in the image of God. We need to be freed of uninformed misunderstandings of Scripture that lay at our feet, the sin of Eve, and thus the fall of the human family. We need to call for an end to poor scriptural scholarship that allows the words and writings attributed to Paul to be used to frustrate the mutuality God intended between men and women.

Jesus freed women and that was radical for his day. He walked with them, ate with them, touched them, listened to them, taught them, loved them, and cut through cultural lines to meet their needs. Sadly, our Christian church has historically gone to great efforts to hide that fact.

You and I have come together in the house of the Lord to celebrate "Women's Sunday." What better place to hold up the lives of hundreds of thousands of women who have contributed to the life of our church? What better place is there to testify to the lives of so many women who have been witnesses of faith and service? Sarah and Rachel, Ruth and Naomi, Mary the mother of the Lord, the bent-over woman, and all those women who walked with the Lord, Catherine of Siena, Theresa of Avila, the medieval mystics, Dorothy Day, Rosa Parks, Bishop Barbara Harris, and we could go on and on...

We come together today to claim our goodness as daughters of the Lord, made in the image of a loving creator, gifted and willing to serve. We come together knowing that it is in mutuality with our brothers that we will help to bring about the kingdom of God in our time and place.

One of the great challenges that will face the Christian church in the coming of the twenty-first century will be whether we have the heart, the will, and the skill to address issues that face women. And these, my brothers and sisters, are issues that have an impact on all of us. Are we ready to address the questions of the feminization of poverty, the plight of single mothers, aging women, and health care? Are we ready to calmly and lovingly dialogue about issues surrounding sexuality, that is, abortion, safe birth control, and sex education? Are we ready to address the place of women in leadership within our churches? Some of our denominations refuse to ordain; others ordain but then jobs are closed to women. Can we address the plight of women of color and our sisters within the Third World?

Ultimately, God's challenge to all of us is to celebrate our gifts and to stand straight and glorify God. Today we urge that for the women of our Christian community, but it is the task of the whole church so that together we can in mutuality serve our God who delights in all of us, male and female. For in us the image of God shines to the world.

Let us together in mutuality and partnership stand together and glorify God.

REFERENCE

Wahlberg, Rachel Conrad. *Jesus and the Freed Woman.* New York: Paulist Press, 1978.

Luke 7:36-50

The Banquet of Forgiveness

Donna Ecker

Preached as a memorial sermon for Tina, who was murdered on the streets of Rochester

One night, two jealous women came to a banquet. It is a banquet that occurs on a weekly basis at Bethany House. A priest is invited, and the word goes out to the highways and byways that all are invited to attend this banquet. Many do come—the beggar, the prophet, the lame, the well, the broken, the healed. All who come are sinners; all who come seek to be forgiven. All who come to the banquet hope to be made whole through the broken bread of the meal. This is a story of forgiveness—of what Jesus Christ calls us to be and do for each other.

On this particular night at the banquet, came two women who hated each other. Their hatred went to the core of their existence, even to the point where each had been arrested for violent acts against the other. This force of emotion came from the root of their hearts—the love of the same man. Now Jimmy is not a young man you would want your daughter to bring home. He is a pimp, a drug dealer, and a user. He is also a charmer with an engaging smile, and he promises the great life is just around the corner.

But I am getting ahead of myself. Let me introduce you to the two women, Linda and Tina. Linda is in her mid-forties with a hefty build, tangled hair, and missing front teeth. She is retarded, unable to read or write, functioning around the level of a ten-year-old. On the best of days, she is obtrusive and loud, unable to set any limits for herself. She spent most of her life institutionalized for her unacceptable behavior. In the mid-70s, when folks were released from mental institutions, Linda was let out in the mainstream with no skills to sustain or maintain a regular lifestyle. Because she has very few life skills, she has failed to adjust and therefore lives on the edge of poverty and desolation.

Tina is a young woman in her mid-twenties who, only a few years ago, had to have been beautiful and ready to take the world by storm. She has long blonde hair, now limp and thin. Her huge brown eyes are now hollow and sad. Tina works the city streets as a hooker, turning as many tricks as possible in a night. You see, she works for Jimmy and shares everything with him—her earnings, her booze, her needles, her bed, her diseases of addiction, and now even AIDS. She loves Jimmy, and she believes that he is her salvation and that their love is paramount. Linda and Tina are in love with the same man, each vying to be the most important in his life.

Jimmy is a manipulator who can charm a lady into poor choices and dangerous lifestyles. Tina has already chosen a dangerous life on the streets for Jimmy. Linda, for all her violent behavior, had led a relatively moral life. Jimmy conned her into letting him and Tina move into Linda's apartment. Before long, the fights started, drugs became a constant problem, and the police were summoned nightly. Ultimately, Linda's belongings were stolen and sold on the street. Linda faced eviction because of the turmoil but did not know how to get them out of her place. She did what she knows best and assaulted them both, getting all of them arrested. They parted company at that point, hating each other and vowing revenge.

Inadvertently, Tina and Linda both came to the banquet at Bethany House on the same night. My heart sank, and my mind filled with terror when they both arrived. I was afraid the banquet was about to turn into a bar-room brawl. As we all gathered around the table, the idea of forgiveness was lost in my fear of impending violence. But something wonderful happened at this meal of sharing. Something truly miraculous happened that night. At the time of petitions of prayer from the community, Linda sat up in her chair and prayed this prayer:

I just wanted to say something here now. I know that Tina and I have been enemies, and I know she hates me, and I know I've hated her. But I'm sorry I've felt that way. I know she's going to have a baby—Jimmy's baby—and I know that they have no place to live. I heard all that on the streets. I'm sorry I beat her up, and I'm sorry I hit Jimmy. I ask God to make this baby okay and that they get a place. It's no good to be pregnant on the streets. I want God to forgive me for the way I behaved, and I want Tina to forgive me, too. Jesus wants us to forgive. He said so. I know we ain't never going to be friends, and that's the way I want it. But we shouldn't be enemies. Amen.

And Jesus said, "Do you see this woman?...I tell you, her sins which are many, are forgiven, for she loved much" (Lk 7:44a, 47a).

Sirach 27:30-28:7
Romans 14:7-9
Matthew 18:21-35

One Woman's Example: Catechetical Sunday

Mary Britton

Today is Catechetical Sunday, and throughout the United States parishes are pausing to remember and celebrate the mission of the church, and therefore of all of us, to preach and teach the good news of Jesus Christ.

As I went about preparing this morning's homily, three words kept repeating themselves over and over in my mind. Two came from the readings today: compassion and forgiveness. The third was catechesis. One of the things I learned last year in a class on preaching is to hone down the focus to one theme or idea and develop that, yet all these words persisted in my heart, and I could not let go of any one of them. Then I ran across the life story of a remarkable woman named Elizabeth Lange, and things seemed to come together.

Elizabeth was born in the early nineteenth century, and as a young woman felt God's call to minister to the poor, especially by educating children and caring for the orphans and the homeless. She wanted to enter religious life and become a sister, but she was refused, all her efforts blocked. You see, Elizabeth was black, and she was living in Baltimore in the 1820s when there was slavery in this country and racism was an accepted way of life. Black men and women were not allowed to enter religious life, and educating slaves was against the law. But Elizabeth held onto her dream, and in 1829 founded the first religious community for African-American women—the Oblate Sisters of Providence. Their purpose was the education and evangelization of African-Americans. Elizabeth was deeply moved by the misery of her people, and she had a tremendous drive to do something about it. So she formed a community of compassion that is still in existence today—mainly in the South—ministering to the poor in education, day care, and other forms of pastoral outreach and social services.

Hers is a powerful story. First, it's a story of forgiveness. What deep pain she must have felt when she was rejected from religious life because of her race. The sting of that rejection must have caused her great anguish. She might have wondered, "How could God allow it?" After all, it was God's work she was trying to do.

Each of us can identify at some level with that kind of pain. We've all experienced hurts, some very deep. We too have wondered, "Where is God in all of this?" And we know how hard it is to forgive. We all have the capacity to be like the unforgiving servant, holding onto the debt, hugging it tight. Forgiveness is a process often requiring a long time as we allow ourselves to face, little by little, and then to feel and work through some very uncomfortable emotions.

We may protect ourselves from hurting by denying the pain: "That doesn't bother me," "I'm not upset...over that...of course not." Then comes anger, which we may have learned is not nice; then the "if only's" of guilt and then sadness. Forgiveness can take a while as we struggle with honest, awkward emotion. It's a healing process. It's how God works with us. I believe that God does not ask the impossible, but that we invite God to be a presence with us in our struggles.

Elizabeth's story is a story of compassion. The dictionary defines compassion as "feeling with" another but going beyond sympathy and empathy to include action. Compassion is dynamic. The psalm today describes our compassionate God as one who pardons, heals, redeems, crowns, and forgives. Elizabeth had compassion for her people, and that provided the energy to drive her to creative action and to forgive those who tried to block her efforts.

Compassion operates in the nooks and crannies of our daily lives. Recently one of the religious education teachers was commenting on the phrase "seventy times seven" (Mt 18:22b) from the Gospel and how hard it can be at times to share your faith. She was an excellent catchiest and spent time preparing her lessons, yet inevitably sooner or later some youngster would say, "This is boring," "I'd rather not be here," or "I already know this." It was her compassion for the kids that kept her going.

Compassion for others takes our faith out of the "church" and into the streets to the hungry, the homeless, the sick, the imprisoned. Our community reaches out with Parish Sharing, education, Take Another Look, evangelization, Pre-Cana, Parish Outreach, ecumenical activity, and so many other ways. People outside our community see our God by what we do. What we do reflects what we believe. That is why Jesus challenges us in the Gospel to be compassionate as he was.

The heart of catechesis then is the ongoing effort to form and reform ourselves into a people of forgiveness and compassion who mirror for the world a forgiving and compassionate God. Through our baptism, we join this community and commit ourselves to this way of life. Catechetical Sunday is an opportunity each year to get focused, challenged, renewed, and committed to following the example of the compassionate Jesus, for, as Paul reminds us, we belong to Jesus. "We are the Lord's" (Rom 14:8b).

How to Be Like Henny Penny

Nancy DeRycke, SSJ

I was at a conference-retreat last weekend on women in the church. We were talking and praying about new opportunities for women and men in the church. It was an exciting time to reflect with other people from around the United States on what is happening and where the Holy Spirit may be guiding us. It was also a scary time because there are so many possibilities, both positive and negative, and it was challenging because the choices we need to make are so crucial.

And then I came home and went to a parish reflection session on Wednesday evening in our parish center where we heard from our "Commitment to Ministry" team. It was a very fine presentation on options to make us an even more vibrant community. The pastor and I were encouraged by the number of interested people who came to hear about ideas dealing with the shortage of priests and using the gifts of individuals and parishes and schools. I know these can be heated topics...

The truth is when we take time to look at what's happening in our church, when we really try to read the signs of the times, it's not always crystal clear; sometimes it's messy. When it isn't clear what's happening or what kind of change may be on the horizon for us, we sometimes get angry or fearful or overwhelmed. We may feel like panicking or giving up or retrenching and refusing to listen to anything.

We can become prophets of doom and disaster like those Jesus refers to in our Gospel today. In point of fact, when Luke's Gospel was written, they had gone through some traumatic events: Jerusalem had been destroyed, there were persecutions, and things weren't progressing as well as the disciples thought they would, and it was clear that Jesus wasn't returning as soon as Paul and others had assumed he would.

We can look around and see our own disasters and wonder if, in fact, the end might be near for us. We think like those who say we are living in the end-times. The world is crashing in around us, and our church is following suit. Maybe it's time we re-examine a moral we learned through a simple story from childhood. Do you remember Chicken Little? Something fell on Chicken Little's head. So Chicken Little decided to go tell the king that the sky was falling in. But first, she told Goosey Lucy, Ducky Lucky, Turkey Lurkey, and Henny Penny. Then they met Foxy Loxy, who said, "I know a shortcut—you can cut through my lair." But as they cut through, Foxy Loxy tricked them and—one by one—gobbled them all up. Only one survived: Henny Penny, who remembered she had to go back and sit on her egg to keep it warm. No one ever told the king that the sky was falling.

The moral of the story? We have to be careful lest we, as Jesus warns us in the Gospel, be deluded by false prophets of doom or rumors. And there are those who feed on rumors and others who are eager to predict when the end is coming. As we get closer to the year 2000, the millenialists will try more and more to convince us. To those of us who can easily get caught up in the rumor or prediction mentality, Jesus says: The important thing is our belief and trust in God! For those who believe, God reminds us that not a single hair on our heads will hurt (Lk 21:18b). (Now I realize that, for some, this is a more significant sign of God's providence than for others!) And God reminds us that "by patience and by your endurance you will gain your lives" (Lk 21:19).

So the Gospel of Luke reminds us of the basic truth of the Christian faith: God's providence and care enfolds us; God never abandons us. And, like Henny Penny, that is the egg we need to sit on in our own lives and keep alive and well: God never abandons us.

Sure, for some of us, there is:

- uncertainty of what's happening in our jobs,

- tension of strained or fragile relationships,

- fear of illness or the progression of a disease, or

- physical limitations as we grow older.

One of the ways we can get through these times is by finding the support of family, loved ones, and parish and, through them, knowing God is with us.But what happens when, as Scripture says, that doesn't happen? What about the Terry Anderson's of the world or others who are held hostage? What do we do when our family deserts us or no one seems to understand and we feel isolated? How do we survive the worst scenarios, when our sky seems to be falling?

Our faith tells us that—*especially even then*—God will not, does not leave us alone. Despite the changes, challenges, and traumas in our world, in our church and in our personal lives, God remains constant.

The sky is falling?

Perhaps.

Or is the sky opening up with challenges to believe in God's providential care as we work and prepare for the coming of the kingdom?

Saints for Today

Deni Mack

Happy All Saints Day! It seems ideal to talk about a few
saints in the context of the Beatitudes, today's Gospel, because it is
saints who live the beatitudes. Trouble is when we talk about
people we've heard are so perfect, we feel uncomfortable, like a
child feels when the teacher keeps talking about an older brother
who got straight A's and whose older sister was an all-state
champion soccer player. The younger child might feel like
"nothing I can do can measure up." We feel that way about saints.
"Nothing we can do can measure up." So let's look at some saintly
people realistically and see some of their shadow sides.

St. Bernadette is reported to have said, "Don't tell me a saint's
virtue, but how they handled their weaknesses." A person's
relationship with God is mysterious. Like a jewel, it deserves to be
examined from many angles.

The first beatitude is "Blessed are the poor in spirit" (Mt 5:3a).
That's dependency on God. We depend on God—so much so that
we pray before, during, and after our work. But we don't all pray the
same way. Here's a shocker: St. Teresa of Lisieux, the little flower,
disliked the rosary! She felt it was an act of faith to fall asleep
during prayer. A contemporary St. Teresa might read the Scriptures
and imagine herself in the story with Jesus and then, while driving
to work, say, "Oh, Jesus, help me treat the people at work the way

you would," and then, during work, say in her heart, "How's it going, Lord? Is this your will?" and listen for the stirrings of the Spirit. Another person might pray the rosary. Somehow it gives me hope when I fall asleep during prayer or reading to know even saints did. Our attitude of dependency on God is basically trusting God; Teresa's attitude was so trusting that she slept. *Blessed are the pure in heart* (Mt 5:8a).

When we look realistically at saints, we find there are worse things than sleeping that saints did: Moses killed a man; David had one killed. Both became sorrowful. Sorrow for sin is saintly. Blessed are the sorrowing, those who mourn. When we are sorry for our sin God does console us; that's the second beatitude.

Our sorrows over injustices to others, our sorrows over deaths and illnesses, all our sorrows are attitudes calling for God's consolation. Sorrow seems to be the attitude God often uses to make us saintly. God heals our attitude. *Blessed are those who mourn* (Mt 5:4a).

A famous French actress[1] felt lonely and sad. She was in need of consolation. She'd felt neglected as a child and when she was eighteen, she saw her father kill her mother and himself. Years later, a parish priest asked her, "Why don't you come to Mass?" She laughed at him. Then she argued with him. They often walked and talked together. Slowly, she realized that she had shut God out of her life. As her attitude opened up to God, her sorrow was consoled. This famous actress simplified her life so that she cared for poor, sick children. God seems to work best when we are sorrowing; we turn to God more; we're open to God; we know we need God more when we are sorrowing. *Blessed are those who mourn* (Mt 5:4a).

The next beatitude is "Blessed are the meek, for they shall inherit the earth" (Mt 5: 5). Saints Isadore and Maria were poor people who loved nature, the feel and smell of newly plowed earth, the first signs of green sprouting each spring. Everything reminded them of God, who creates the world and everything in it. Saint Isadore is the patron saint of farmers. Isadore and Maria might also be considered patron saints of parents of children who died from SIDS (Sudden Infant Death Syndrome) as their baby died. This couple could neither read nor write, yet they were admired and respected. Juan de Varga, the landowner whose land they worked, had money, education, a mansion with servants, and a large farm, but he felt that Maria and Isadore were happier and more generous than he was. Isadore and Maria shared the little that they had with people even poorer than they were. *Blessed are the meek* (Mt 5:5a) and *Blessed are those who hunger and thirst for righteousness* (Mt 5:6a).

A black woman, Mary McLeod Bethune, was saintly in her single-hearted pursuit of education for African-American children. Bethune was saintly in her ability to be merciful even though she had been treated unmercifully as a child. She was born just one hundred years ago in a small town; the white people there would not permit her in school and made her put down the book when she wanted to learn to read. She cried. A few years later, when Mary's church opened a school, a teacher came to the cotton fields to find the students. There, Mary learned to read the Bible to her proud parents. Later, Mary founded a school in Florida, and her work became so well-known that President Franklin D. Roosevelt called her to Washington. Mary McLeod Bethune was the first black woman to be in charge of a federal agency. Thousands of people are well educated because one day the daughter of former slaves made up her mind she would learn to read. She was single hearted in her pursuit of education for her people. *Blessed are the merciful* (Mt 5:7a). *Blessed are those who hunger and thirst for righteousness* (Mt 5:6a).

Saint Jane Francis de Chantal's mother died when she was eighteen months old. When she was in her twenties, Jane was widowed. She was raising four children and managing a large farm. But for four months after her husband died, Jane could hardly cope because she was so depressed. Her father-in-law was furious with her. His housekeeper made life very difficult for Jane and her children.

De Chantal and Francis de Sales became very close friends. They worked together with their problems, hopes, and dreams and founded the first order of women religious who did not stay in the convent all the time. They are more like Sister Marie,[2] out visiting the sick.

But please remember that de Chantal's depression nearly got the best of her; Mary McLeod Bethune and the French actress were treated unmercifully as children. The "Little Flower" disliked the rosary; Isadore and Maria could not read.

None of these people were perfect. Far from it. They weren't making peace twenty-four hours a day. They were fully human, aware of their imperfections. But they each allowed God to heal their attitudes. They were insulted; some were persecuted; but they tried, with God's help, to let go of the grudges they might have carried. They each had shadow sides they did not let control them. We too can accept the fact that we simply cannot be perfect, but we can with God's help be saints. You are saints. On our parish council retreat last summer, we were asked who are the saints that inspire us, and several council members named parishioners; some named their own parents and spouses, who really tried to heal wounds and communicate better and understand more.

Saints weren't all serious. St. Teresa of Avila reformed the Carmelite convents and really effected a reformation of church corruption as did St. Catherine of Siena, who told the pope to get back to Rome. A stained glass window of Teresa shows her dancing. Saints aren't only serious; they appreciate the great joy in their lives. Some say the beatitudes, or blessings, can be translated as "happy" as in "happy are the poor in spirit," (Mt 5:3a), "happy are the merciful," (Mt 5:7a), and "happy are the peacemakers" (Mt 5:9a). Happy All Saints Day. May your attitude be a happy one as God richly blesses you, releasing the saint in you.

NOTES

1. Stories about Mary McLeod Bethune, Francis de Chantal, Isadore and Marie, and Eve LaValliere, a French actress, are all found in Janaan Manternach and Carl J. Pfeifer's book *People to Remember* (New York: Paulist Press, 1987).
2. Sister Marie Martin Quinn, to whom this book is dedicated.

Isaiah 62:1-5
1 Corinthians 12:4-11
John 2:1-12

Don't Hide Your Gifts in Drawers!

Nancy Giordano

When I was a little girl, probably somewhere between the ages of six and eight years old, I remember our family received a package in the mail. This was quite unusual, a real event. Inside the package there was a gift for me. I was very excited to open it and to find that my aunt had sent me a pair of pink pajamas. They were beautiful—a soft satiny material with blue piping around the lapel and pocket—like nothing I had ever had before. I was thrilled and ready to wear them that very night.

But my mother had other ideas. She and my Dad had lived through the hard years of the Depression, and she knew the value of saving for a rainy day. She reminded me that we were to visit my aunt that very summer, and my nice new pj's would be perfect for that special occasion. So we folded them back up and put them in *her* dresser drawer, so I wouldn't be tempted to wear them. We saved them. And after awhile, I forgot about them, and so did she.

Those pajamas were a special gift, given to me to enjoy. Gifts are given to be used and enjoyed by the receiver; often they are gifts that can be shared with others, and when shared, often bring us greater pleasure.

In today's Scripture, Paul speaks to the community at Corinth about the gifts of the spirit—the powers and abilities which the spirit bestows on all. They are different gifts, each one suited to the

person who receives it, and each gift is not meant to be used solely
by the receiver, for him or her alone, but for *the common good*. The
church at Corinth was given everything it needed—like our church.
Though the gifts are different—leadership, hospitality,
peacemaking, preaching, proclaiming God's word—gifts are given
for each ministry and each need of the community—each gift is
special and tailor-made to fit perfectly the person to whom it is
given. No gift makes a person better or is to be held in higher
esteem. All are perfect gifts, given by the perfect giver, and meant
to be *enjoyed, used, shared*, for the good of all.

God's gracious love for us is manifested in no greater gift than
the gift of God's son. Jesus is the most generous outpouring of
God's love given to the world. Jesus, tucked away, hidden, living a
quiet life for about thirty years, now begins at Cana, at the urging of
his mother, to let the world know who he is, to manifest his divine
nature, and to pour out God's love for humanity like wine poured
out for all to drink, to enjoy and to share. His miracle at Cana is the
occasion in John's Gospel for his disciples to begin believing in
Jesus, to see him as a wonder worker who can turn water in stone
jars into choice wine worthy of a wedding feast.

Water turned to wine. Wine is a sign of the new covenant, a new
era between God and humanity. Wine is the remembrance of
Christ's blood poured out for us, when his hour had come, in the
self-giving sacrifice, the saving action on the cross. Wine, the blood
of Christ, offered to us each Sunday at our eucharistic feast. Wine—
given at a marriage feast—the symbol of the great banquet to be
celebrated in the final days when the fulfillment of the kingdom
has come and where we live forever in joy with our God.

God offers us so many gifts: material gifts and spiritual gifts, the
things we have—the abilities and talents which are ours, the faith
we have—the recognition of God's tremendous love for us. All of
these are gifts which are meant to be received, cherished, and
shared. Do we recognize the gifts God gives us? Do we use them for
the good of all—our families, our church, our poor, our world? Or do
we hoard them for a future that may never come, keeping them just
for ourselves?

Each day, each moment, God gives us gifts, gifts that are
necessary for that day, gifts that are suitable for that moment. Like
ordinary water in stone jars, God can change *us* into choice wine,
transforming our lives by the power of love and gifts, turning us

ordinary people into something extraordinary, turning us into choice wine to be poured out, shared by all.

Oh, yes—what about my pajamas? That summer, when the time for our trip arrived, I remembered my pajamas. We took them from my mother's drawer, unfolded them, and held them up to see if they needed pressing, and we were amazed. Here were my beautiful pajamas—still shiny and pink and new. I tried them on to discover my arms hanging out far below the sleeves, my legs sticking out—the pj's stopping inches short of my ankles. During the months since receiving them, I had grown, and they had stayed the same. I had outgrown them without ever having the joy of wearing them. For me, they were a gift that was never used—wasted.

Don't let that happen to your gifts! Don't let the love, the talent, the gifts God gives you be wasted. When the time is right, put your gifts on. Use them. Pour them out—for your good—for the good of all!

Proverbs 31:10-13,19-20,30-31
1 Thessalonians 5:1-6
Matthew 25:14-30

What Do We Bury in Fear?

Marie Susanne Hoffman, SSJ

Preached at University of Rochester Chapel

In his book *One Generation After* (New York: Schocken Books, 1965), Nobel prize winner Elie Wiesel told a story he entitled "The Watch." At the time of his Bar Mitzvah, he received a watch which became especially treasured. In April 1944, the town in which he was living decided to expel all of its Jewish citizens so that the Nazis would spare the town. Many of the Jews who were about to be driven out decided to bury their treasures in the hope that the Nazi madness would pass and they would be able to return to their village and reclaim their treasures. Elie Wiesel buried his watch in a spot he had carefully measured off from a fence and a tree.

Twenty years later, he returned home as one of the few concentration camp survivors from that village. He measured off the distance from the tree and fence and began to dig with his bare hands until the outlines of a box emerged. In the box, was the treasured watch, now sadly ruined. After studying it for a while, he returned it to its hiding place in the hope that another might find it someday and learn that among the inhabitants of that town, once upon a time, there had been Jews and Jewish children robbed of their future.

That poignant story is a critique of more than one small town in Eastern Europe in the 1940s. It is a story of all humanity, both communally and individually. Just as Wiesel's town tried to bury the fact that Jews were living there by expelling them, so have certain societal structures and attitudes tried to bury those who are different so that their presence could not be an embarrassment. In so doing, individuals and groups of people have been robbed of their future. For years, children with Downs Syndrome were whisked away from their families and placed in institutions so that their parents wouldn't have to face the gossip of neighbors and relatives. For years, white communities tried to bury the fact that blacks existed by barring them from neighborhoods, schools, stores, and a whole range of opportunities for advancement. For years, families who had someone with a chemical dependency covered up the person's behavior and made all kinds of excuses so that no one would know that the person needed intervention and treatment. Today, many families bury the fact that someone has AIDS for fear of the harsh judgments that would be made about that person's lifestyle.

We have been buried through a literal interpretation of the Scriptures that does not take into account the cultural and historical milieu in which readings like today's first reading have to be situated in order for us to be able to hear God's message to us today. We have been buried by social stereotypes of women as second-class citizens, as intellectually inferior, as temptresses, as cheap labor. Many women have been buried under economic pressure; one third of female-headed families live in poverty. Finally, the drafts of the Bishops' Pastoral on Women acknowledge that women have been buried by the institutional church to the extent that we have not been included in the church's liturgical, administrative, and pastoral life.

In today's Gospel, the action of burying was done by an individual who was trying to play it safe. The servant was motivated by fear of his master's personality. His actions cost him his hope for the future. What the Gospel tells us about the servant presents each of us with a challenge. When we look at our lives, what do we bury out of fear? What might the consequences be?

Do we bury our emotions, our spontaneity, because if we allow our emotions to surface we may no longer be in control and we can't deal with not being in control? Do we bury our sense of adventure and risk-taking because it's just too unsettling to attempt the unknown and we don't like to open ourselves up to the possibility of failure? Do we bury what we'd like to study or the work we'd like to do because our family and all our friends expect us to be doctors, lawyers, physicists, chemical engineers, and we're afraid of everyone's reaction if we say, "But that's not what I want to do!"? Do we bury our rounds of loneliness with rounds of drinking, drugs, or casual sex because we are afraid to face what every human being experiences at some time in life—the pain of being alone? Do we bury laughter and joy because we are in higher education, which is serious business and we won't be taken seriously if we show that we have a sense of humor? Do we bury our need for others because we're afraid that others will think we can't stand on our own two feet and be as self-reliant as society dictates we should be? Do we bury the deepest need we have as human beings, the need for God, because we're afraid to let others know that we have a sneaking suspicion that there may be more to this religion business than getting in here on Sunday and getting out of here as soon as possible?

To risk losing part of human life, to risk losing part of our future because of fear is a terrible burden to carry and in the case of a Christian is an unnecessary burden as well. The master in today's Gospel was a harsh man, but our God is not harsh. Certainly, God expects us to be willing to take a risk. In the Gospel parable, those who risked were rewarded. But the risk we are asked to take is grounded in the certainty of who our God is. In the First Letter of John we read, "There is no fear in love, but perfect love casts out fear" (1 Jn 4:18a). There could be no better example of perfect love than the example we have been given in Jesus, an example which should encourage us to bring our fears to God so that God's love can give us the courage to stop burying part of our lives, to uncover what we've hidden, so that we can live the truly human lives God calls us to live. Let us walk in the love which casts out fear and leave behind our hiding, stereotyping, and burying.

PART 4

Recessional

We've Only Just Begun...

Marie Martin Quinn, RSM

Sr. Marie Martin Quinn's homily on facing death was preached in October 1981.

Scarcely a week goes by that we don't know of a friend, acquaintance, a relative, or close family member that has died. Yet somehow death, with all its frequency, never becomes a common, taken-for-granted occurrence. It invariably takes us by surprise even in cases of terminal illness. Our natural reaction to death is usually shock and disbelief and perhaps fear and distaste.

All phases of earthly life have their beginnings and ends. Conception and birth begin the human life cycle, followed by periods of growth and development, blooming, maturing, and dying. This last week we watched (first hand) flowers and trees in their dying stage— nature dying in all her glory of color. Life after death, eternity, is difficult for our minds to comprehend; this timelessness frightens us.

As science makes new discoveries that deal with human life, we seem the more to fear and try to deny the reality of death. Some record for us the many people who have been declared clinically dead and have returned to life to tell us what the interval was like. Our desires to have a fuller understanding of death are only human. Perhaps because we are so much a part of this life, it's hard for us to imagine much happiness once our body is dead. Or perhaps we think the soul is so bound up with the body that it's unthinkable to go on existing apart from it. No one has ever come back to tell us about life after death. I'm sure it's because this new life is so wonderful that those who have died have no desire to return.

At present, we are like someone with a few pieces of a jigsaw puzzle. In our afterlife, the puzzle will be completed and be a picture of immense beauty and love. How can we begin to come to a deeper and fuller understanding of death and resurrection?

We who live in and with Christ are prepared to die with and in him. The more we have loved in this life, the greater will be our love and happiness in the next. Death is something we should be preparing for all during life, but so few want to even think of it, let alone prepare for it. The time of the death of someone we love is a good time for reflecting on our own lives, reevaluating life's purposes, and acknowledging that our time will come, too. The more we can talk about Christian death and its inevitability, the less fear it causes. We can come to understand that death is truly the beginning of the fulfillment of life with God.

How can we ready ourselves for this encounter? We can continually grow in a personal relationship with God through daily prayer—sometimes just listening to God in the quiet of our heart. We can pray the Scriptures. They assure us about the life to come. We are very good about praying for others' needs, but we need also to pray often for a peaceful and happy death for ourselves.

The sacraments, especially the Eucharist and Penance, and reaching out to one another in love, are fine ways of being always ready. We really identify with Christ when we can accept the disappointments and hurts of this life.

As baptized Catholics, we have committed ourselves to follow Christ and move along on life's journey in a deepening awareness of God working in us. What a sad Christian who spends life just going through the motions!

Each day we need to pray for confidence in God's love for us. Christ wants all people to be saved. He died that we may live. Our life needs to be a daily preparation—a longing for our meeting with God and with our loved ones. How fortunate we are to believe in the resurrection of the body and life everlasting. We have *hope* for a far, far better life than we have ever known here. Heaven is really living at last.

Our Scriptures this weekend call us to a readiness and to a growing desire to be with the Lord unceasingly. If we have any doubts about God's love and longing for you and me, just recall the lines from St. Paul: Eye has not seen, ear has not heard, nor has the human heart received, what God has prepared for those who love God (1 Cor 2:9).

About the Contributors

Roni Antenucci holds an MA degree in theology (ministry studies) from St. Bernard's Institute and is currently working on her MDiv degree at St. Bernard's. She has worked as a pastoral care associate at St. Ann's Home in Rochester and is currently a pastoral associate at Our Lady of Mercy in Greece, New York. She is married and the mother of three grown children.

Sandra Clark Arrington holds an MDiv degree from St. Bernard's Institute and has done supplemental work in Anglican Studies at Bexley Hall. In 1994 she was ordained an Episcopal priest. She is married and has three grown children and one grandchild. Currently, she is associate rector at St. Paul's Episcopal Church in Rochester.

Mary Britton is diocesan catechetical consultant for the Diocese of Rochester. She holds an MA degree in theology from St. Bernard's Institute and has done graduate work in education at Syracuse University. She is a member of Rochester Women's Ordination Conference and the National Conference of Catechetical Leadership. She is married, the mother of three children and the grandmother of one.

Nancy DeRycke is a Sister of St. Joseph and currently serving as the parish administrator of St. Helen's Church in Rochester. She holds an MDiv degree from St. Bernard's Institute and has been in pastoral ministry for more than twenty years. She has been active on the Commission on Women in the Church, Society of the Rochester Diocese, and Rochester Women's Ordination Conference.

Donna Ecker is the director of Bethany House, a shelter for homeless women, and an associate of the Sisters of Mercy. She holds a certificate in theology from St. Bernard's Institute. She is married and the mother of four grown children and grandmother of four. Donna also ministers at St. Joseph's Church in Penfield with her husband, Tom, a deacon.

Toinette M. Eugene is associate professor of Christian social ethics at Garrett-Evangelical Theological Seminary and a member of the graduate faculty of Northwestern University in Evanston, Illinois. She holds an MA in Theology and Education from the Jesuit School of Theology at Berkeley and a PhD in religion and society from the Graduate Theological Union. She is a former member of the faculty and provost of Colgate Rochester Divinity School, Bexley Hall, Crozer Theological Seminary in Rochester, New York. Abingdon Press is publishing her two forthcoming books, *Lifting As We Climb: A Womanist Ethic of Care* and, with James N. Poling, *Balm for Gilead: Pastoral Care for African-American Families Experiencing Abuse*. She is an avid photographer and accomplished potter. She is learning the art of African-American quilting as a way of reclaiming and rejoicing in her womanist roots and relationships.

Nancy Giordano is the pastoral associate at St. Ambrose in Rochester. She holds an MA degree in theology from St. Bernard's Institute. She has been active on the Rochester Liturgical Commission and is presently serving on the Board of Trustees for St. Bernard's Institute. She is married and the mother of five children.

Kay Heverin is a Sister of St. Joseph. She is currently pastoral associate at Sacred Heart Cathedral in Rochester. She has a Master's degree in religious education from Loyola University in Chicago. She is active in ministry within the gay and lesbian community through Dignity/Integrity Rochester.

Marie Susanne Hoffman is a Sister of St. Joseph and former director of campus ministry for the Diocese of Rochester. She served as a chaplain at the University of Rochester. She presently serves as pastoral associate at St. Charles Borromeo Parish in Rochester. She holds an MA degree in theology (Scripture) from St. Bernard's Institute. She was active on the Commission on Women in the Church and Society and is currently on a Rochester Diocese Synod Implementation Committee for Faith Development.

Roslyn A. Karaban is a tenured associate professor of ministry studies at St. Bernard's Institute and a pastoral counselor at Samaritan Pastoral

Counseling Center, both in Rochester. She has an MDiv degree from Harvard Divinity School and a PhD in religion and the personality sciences from the Graduate Theological Union. She served as coordinator of Rochester Women's Ordination Conference from 1990 to 1993. She has a number of articles and homilies published, with her primary focus being on cross-cultural counseling and lay women. She has another book forthcoming, *Six Steps to Discerning God's Call* (Resource Publications, Inc., 1997). She is married and the mother of two children. Her hobbies include running, aerobics, and kung fu.

Yvonne Lucia is presently involved with doing retreat work and adult education seminars on women's issues and spirituality. She was formerly an instructor in the Formation for Ministry Program, diocese of Syracuse, and a facilitator for the Loyola Institute of Ministry Extension program. She holds a BS degree in nursing from the University of Rochester and an MDiv degree from Colgate Rochester Divinity School/Bexley Hall/Crozer Theological Seminary. She is married and the mother of four children.

Deni (Denise Winfield) Mack is the pastoral associate at St. Gregory's in Marion and St. Anne's in Palmyra, New York. She has an MA in theology (Scripture) and an MDiv degree, both from St. Bernard's. She also holds a DMin degree in spirituality from Colgate Rochester Divinity School/ Bexley Hall/Crozer Theological Seminary in collaboration with St. Bernard's Institute. In 1989 she was among the first women to receive an award from St. Bernard's for being an Outstanding Catholic Woman. She is married, the mother of four, and the grandmother of six.

Barbara Moore is a Sister of Mercy who has studied at the Theological Consortium in Washington, DC. She holds an MA in American History from the University of Rochester and an MDiv degree from Colgate Rochester Divinity School, Bexley Hall, Crozer Theological Seminary. She was the director of Interfaith Jail Ministries from 1980 to 1990 and also served as community liaison for Health and Human Services for Congresswoman Louise M. Slaughter. She is presently a community services coordinator for Highland Hospital in Rochester and active in an interfaith ministry of preaching.

Marie Martin Quinn was a Sister of Mercy who served St. Rita's Parish in Webster, New York, as pastoral associate from 1979 until Thanksgiving Day 1991, when she returned to the home God had prepared for her. After many years of teaching and service as an elementary school principal, Sister Marie found her call in parish ministry, and for that the people of St. Rita's are forever grateful. Her life was one of prayerful thanksgiving. This book is dedicated to her.

Martha Ann Sims is a laywoman, married and the mother of five children and grandmother of one child. She spent her childrearing years working in the areas of elementary and secondary education as well as volunteering in school, parish, and youth activities. She completed an MDiv from St. Bernard's Institute in 1992 and afterward worked as a pastoral associate at St. Charles Borromeo Parish and as an adjunct chaplain at Strong Memorial Hospital in Rochester. She has served on the commissions for Women in the Church and Society and for Ecumenism in the Rochester Diocese. Presently she is working on a Master of Social Work degree at Washington University in St. Louis, Missouri.

Joan Sobala is a Sister of St. Joseph and the senior pastoral associate at St. Mary's Church in Rochester. She holds an MDiv degree from St. Bernard's Seminary and an MA in mathematics from the University of Notre Dame. She taught for ten years in the women's studies program at Nazareth College. She was one of the founders of the Rochester Regional Task Force on Women in the Church and an editor and founder of the WOC publication, *New Women/New Church*. From 1979 to 1982 she was a staff member of WOC, and for seven years she co-hosted a Sunday morning radio program called *Good Morning, God*. She is currently the coordinator of Rochester Women's Ordination Conference.

Theresa Stanley is a chaplain at Southport Correctional Facility, the only disciplinary special housing unit in New York state. She is the first laywoman to be appointed to this kind of facility in New York state. She has a background in teaching and holds an MS degree in education from Elmira College. She also holds an MA degree in pastoral studies from Loyola in New Orleans. She conducts various types of retreats and is a facilitator for faith development. She is involved with disability issues nationally. She is married and the mother of three children.

Mary C. Sullivan is a Sister of Mercy and professor of language and literature at Rochester Institute of Technology (RIT). She holds a Master of Theology degree from the University of London and an MA and PhD in English from the University of Notre Dame. She is a former dean of the College of Liberal Arts at RIT and was a member of the Board of Trustees at St. Bernard's Institute for twelve years. She is a published author in her field and has served on numerous committees in the Sisters of Mercy and in the Diocese of Rochester.

Gloria Ulterino is pastoral associate at St. Joseph Church and at St. William Church in Livonia and Conesus, New York. She has an MA degree in theology from St. Bernard's Institute, and she is completing her MDiv degree at St. Bernard's. She has been in pastoral ministry for the last ten years, including four months as a temporary pastoral administrator. She has been active on the Commission on Women in the Church and the Society. She is married and the mother of three children.

Index of Scripture References

Genesis 3:9-15,26 . . . . Immaculate Conception 15

Exodus 17:3-7 . . . . 3rd Sunday of Lent (A) 26

Ruth 1:8-18 61

Proverbs 31:10-13,19-20,30-31 . . 33rd Sunday of the Year (C) 81

Isaiah 55:1-3 . . . . 18th Sunday of the Year (A) 3
Isaiah 62:1-5 . . . . 2nd Sunday of the Year (C) 78

Sirach 27:30-28:7 . . . . 24th Sunday of the Year (A) 68

Matthew 5:1-12 . . . . All Saints 74
Matthew 14:13-21 . . . . 18th Sunday of the Year (A) 3
Matthew 15:21-28 . . . . 20th Sunday of the Year (A) 29
Matthew 18:21-35 . . . . 24th Sunday of the Year (A) 68
Matthew 25:14-30 . . . . 33rd Sunday of the Year (C) 81

Mark 14:3-9 52

Luke 1:26-38 . . . . Immaculate Conception 15, 23
Luke 1:39-45 . . . . 4th Sunday of Advent (C) 49
Luke 7:36-50 65
Luke 8:40-56 6

Luke 10:38-42. 43
Luke 10:38-42. . . . . Tuesday of the 27th Week of the Year (II) 46
Luke 13:10-17. . . . . 32, 61
Luke 21:5-19. . . . . 33rd Sunday of the Year (C) 71

John 2:1-12 . . . . 2nd Sunday of the Year (C). 78
John 4:5-42 . . . . 3rd Sunday of Lent (A) 26
John 8:1-11 . . . . 5th Sunday of Lent (C) 38
John 11:1-27 43

Acts 5:27-32. 6

Romans 5:1-2,5-8 . . . . 3rd Sunday of Lent (A) 26
Romans 8:35,37-39. . . . . 18th Sunday of the Year (A) 3
Romans 14:7-9 . . . . 24th Sunday of the Year (A) 68

1 Corinthians 12:4-11. . . . . 2nd Sunday of the Year (C). 78

1 Thessalonians 5:1-6. . . . . 33rd Sunday of the Year (C) 81